THE GLASGOW STYLE

THE GLASGOW STYLE

GERALD AND CELIA LARNER

WITH PHOTOGRAPHS BY
VICTOR ALBROW
AND STEVEN DANIELS

TAPLINGER PUBLISHING COMPANY
New York

First published in the United States in 1979
by TAPLINGER PUBLISHING CO., INC
New York

Library of Congress Catalog Card Number: 78–20694

ISBN 0–8008–3274–4

Printed by Robert MacLehose and Company Limited
Printers to the University of Glasgow
Renfrew, near Glasgow, Scotland

CONTENTS

ACKNOWLEDGEMENTS

Our thanks are due, firstly, to the Glasgow-style collectors who so patiently suffered domestic upheaval for the sake of our photography. Some of them prefer to remain anonymous but most of them are identified, with the photographer, below or alongside the appropriate illustration. We are also indebted to those institutions—University of Glasgow Art Collections, Glasgow Art Gallery, Victoria & Albert Museum, Walker Art Gallery (Liverpool) and Museum Bellerive (Zurich)—who supplied us with their own photographs. Sotheby's Belgravia has been a valuable source of material and we are grateful to Peter Nahum of Sotheby's paintings department as well as to Roger Billcliffe of the Fine Arts Society, Patrick Bourne of Steigal Fine Art, Cordelia Oliver, Ruth White, and Michael Whiteway for their help in tracing certain objects and photographs.

Our gratitude is not exhausted by these particular acknowledgements and, indeed, since this book is only a preliminary survey of a very fascinating field of study, we would be happy to learn new facts and examine more Glasgow-style objects as they come to light. We can be contacted through our ever helpful publisher, Paul Harris.

THE GLASGOW STYLE

The creator and indisputable master of the Glasgow style was Charles Rennie Mackintosh. There was no more progressive architect or designer working in Britain round the turn of the century and none more inspired in Europe. It is not inconceivable, however, that Glasgow would have become a centre of the decorative arts at that time even without his influence. The talent, the commercial motivation, the visual awareness, the teachers, and the craftsmen were all there. Although Glasgow without his innovatory genius might not have developed its own characteristic style in design, its arts and crafts would certainly have flourished, and possibly with more colour and more poetry than the contemporary English version.

Without Mackintosh, Miss Cranston would have continued to build her chain of distinctively decorated tea rooms. Even without the encouragement of international admiration for a young Glasgow architect, it is not unlikely that enterprising furnishers like Wylie & Lochhead would have retained their own local designers—at least for the 1901 Exhibition—as well as retailing chairs and hall furniture from Baillie Scott's manufacturers in Bedford and art nouveau cabinets from London. The stained glass industry in the workshops of J. & W. Guthrie and Oscar Paterson, among others, would have flourished no less.

Certainly, there was a demand for modern furnishings in a city where the interest in contemporary art—carefully cultivated by the far-seeing dealer, Alex Reid—was at least as advanced as anywhere else in Britain. The taste of well endowed Scottish collectors embraced not only the Barbizon and Hague schools but also the French impressionists (first introduced to Glasgow by Reid in 1892) and the local heroes, the Glasgow Boys. The influence of these Glasgow painters on the development of the decorative arts was considerable, though more in the creation of a favourable atmosphere than in the creation of imagery. They had proved that it was possible to win international fame without first being recognised by the Establishment in London or even being elected to the Royal Scottish Academy in Edinburgh. John Lavery, James Paterson and Alexander Roche all gained awards at the Paris Salon before being elected to the RSA, and it was only after the enormous success of the Glasgow Boys in the Munich Exhibition of 1890 that they were accorded general acceptance in Edinburgh.

Two of the major characteristics of the Glasgow school of painting are its decorative quality and its bold use of colour. As a German critic of the time observed, 'There burst out a style of painting which took its origin altogether from decorative harmony and the rhythms and forms of masses of colour.' If there was a danger that this kind of work might, as the same critic put it, 'approach the border where painting ends and the Persian carpet begins', designers of carpets could at least learn something from it.

In one or two cases, indeed, the Glasgow painters not only inspired the designers with a feeling for colour but also supplied them with their imagery. *The Druids: Bringing in the Mistletoe*, which E. A. Hornel and George Henry worked on together in 1890, is a painting of exceptional significance in this respect. It took a Mackintosh to realise its full implications, but by 1896 another Glasgow school artist, David Gauld, had converted it into a stained glass window design. It was David Gauld—a friend of Mackintosh, incidentally—who in about 1889 had painted the remarkable *St Agnes*: its solitary, elongated figure in the centre foreground, its composition in patches of colour, the flattened perspective of the landscape in the background, all make it look almost like a study for a Glasgow style embroidery ten years before its time.

What Mackintosh found in *The Druids*—and he must have seen the painting, even though there is no record of it being exhibited in Glasgow in the 1890s—was not the Celtic decoration on the robes and accoutrements of the priests in the foreground but something much more profoundly atavistic. It was the tall, straight-backed, stiff-necked druidic ritual figures which he later transferred to posters, transformed into chairs, and forged into wrought-iron totems. The Glasgow designers were, with a few exceptions, curiously uninterested in the entrelacs and the ring and snake motifs of Celtic decoration. Although there was a revival of the Celtic tradition in Scotland, it was an East-coast preoccupation, promoted above all by Patrick Geddes, editor of the *Evergreen*. Since only four numbers of the *Evergreen* were published, in Edinburgh between 1895 and 1897, its influence was limited. But it contained some strikingly stylish illustrations by Robert Burns and strongly symbolic compositions by John Duncan—many of them Celtic in derivation and at the same time art nouveau in spirit—between aptly decorative covers by Charles H. Mackie.

Perhaps the most interesting examples of the Celtic revival in Scotland are the watercolours of John Duncan's young colleague in Dundee, George Dutch Davidson, and the jewellery and silver work of James Cromer Watt, the Aberdeen enamellist who exhibited in the Scottish section at Turin in 1902 and on several later occasions in Glasgow and Edinburgh. It is unfortunate that this almost exclusively two-dimensional talent could not be applied to furniture or building design by an Edinburgh equivalent of, say, Baillie Scott who so usefully developed a feeling for Celtic ornament from his association with Archibald Knox on the Isle of Man in the 1890s. Robert Lorimer, though sympathetic to the arts and crafts, was not that kind of architect.

GEORGE WALTON To return to Glasgow, the most convincing indication that the time was ripe for a flowering of the decorative arts in that city—with or without Charles Rennie Mackintosh—was the, on the face of it, extraordinary decision of George Walton at the age of twenty-one to throw over his job as a bank clerk and set himself up as a designer and decorator. This was in 1888, when Mackintosh was still an apprentice in the offices of John Hutchinson and a student at evening classes in the School of Art. The immediate prospect for Walton in 1888 was apparently the chance to decorate a smoking room at 114 Argyle Street, which Miss Cranston had first opened as a tea room in 1884. But that was scarcely a career. On the other hand, as the younger brother of E. A. Walton, one of the Glasgow Boys, he must have been aware of the atmosphere in the artistic community at the time and must have been excited by it. He would have been aware, too, of the growing demand, in a restricted but well funded circle of Glasgow connoisseurs, for contemporary works of art.

Walton was not himself a painter—though he had attended evening art classes—but the aesthetic movement had made the practice of decorative design culturally respectable and even desirable. Holman Hunt, Ford Maddox Brown and D. G. Rossetti had all designed chairs; Burne Jones designed stained glass, tapestries, and even jewellery; and Whistler's decorative schemes were, according to Walton himself, 'the most remarkable event of his time'. Some of Walton's best known and most characteristic furnishings derive, in fact, from the aesthetic movement. He was never totally committed to the arts and crafts or to art nouveau and, though eclectic in style and variable in achievement, he developed a kind of elegance peculiar to himself. It is difficult to believe that his slender aesthetic style ebonised chair and his broad-bottomed country-style arm chair could have been designed by the same hand for the same patron at the same time. And yet the perilously out-curved front legs of the one and the unsupported arms of the other exercise a similar structural fascination.

Whatever Walton's reasons for setting himself up as a decorator, they were proved right. By 1896 his reputation—based largely on his stencilled wallpapers—was such that it was to him that Miss Cranston turned when she came to furnish her ambitious new tea rooms in Buchanan

Street. He designed a surprisingly modern hoarding of Whistlerian extravagance for the outside of the shop during alterations, and a handsome billiard room with the country-style chairs and matching tables, a brightly painted tapestry-like frieze of medieval hunting scenes, and imaginative light fittings over the billiard table. Some of his furniture, however, looks disappointingly conventional in the photographs, most of all that which has to compete with the murals of his young collaborator, C. R. Mackintosh, and the hat racks so ingeniously designed as an additional dimension to the stencilled wall decorations behind them.

Perhaps this is why in 1897, when Miss Cranston went on to extend and reconstruct her tea rooms in Argyle Street, the rôles were reversed: Mackintosh was responsible for all the furniture except the billiard tables and Walton for the wall and ceiling decoration, fireplaces and light fittings. This, in its turn, might explain why Walton, finding himself no longer the most favoured of progressive designers in Glasgow, left for London in 1898. There were other possible reasons, such as that his wife had come from London and that his painter brother had successfully settled there four years earlier. Moreover, unlike Mackintosh, Walton did not need a Scottish background to sustain his imagination. Much of his inspiration derived from England, first from Morris & Co. and later from Voysey, and he had never had any difficulty in pleasing his English clients. He had designed tea-room interiors in Scarborough for Rowntree & Sons in 1896 and 1897 and he had enough business in Yorkshire to open a shop in Stonegate, York, in 1898—the year in which he furnished Elm Bank on The Mount.

In London discreet touches of the post-Mackintosh Glasgow style in his carpets and his furniture for Liberty and J. S. Henry combined with his own characteristic elegance to make him one of the most successful of commercial designers. His refitting in about 1900 of the chain of Kodak shops, extending from London to Brussels, Milan and Vienna, carried his name and influence abroad. Several foreign commissions followed, perhaps the most flattering being the living room for an exhibition of fifteen interiors on the premises of the Berlin furnishers, A. S. Ball, in 1905. Mackintosh contributed a dining room to the same exhibition.

It is a mark of Walton's success in London that as early as 1901 he was asked to design his first house, The Leys at Elstree. Having previously been responsible only for interiors, shop fronts and exhibition stands, he nevertheless completed a large, satisfyingly symmetrical building which, though unadventurous, was competent enough to bring him more architectural commissions. His most ambitious domestic undertakings were Wern Fawr at Harlech (1907) and the White House at Shiplake (1908). Even in the smaller houses, like The Philippines at Brasted in Kent and Alma House, Cheltenham, the interiors were tastefully and resourcefully designed to combine conventional ideas of quality with Walton's own style. The dignified and yet informal cabinet designed in 1902 for The Philippines is—with its gilded, distinctly Glasgow-derived squares under the cornice, its curved glass sides and tapering supports— a particularly attractive example of his upper-middle manner. If there is nothing distinctively Scottish in his Clutha glass vases (though made in Glasgow by J. Couper & Sons) and the Powell glass tableware he designed for these houses, there is certainly a strong Glasgow flavour in the Cawdor candlestick in the White House and the light fittings such as those which illuminate the billiard table at The Leys.

HERBERT MACNAIR George Walton was not the only promising designer to leave Glasgow in 1898. Herbert MacNair left at the same time and for the same possible reason—the awareness that any other progressive young Glasgow architect was bound to be overshadowed by the genius of Charles Rennie Mackintosh, whose masterpiece, the new School of Art, was already being built at this time. MacNair and Mackintosh had probably known each other for ten years by then, since it was in 1888 that MacNair was articled to John Honeyman and, as part of his training, began to attend the same evening classes at the School of Art. In 1889 Mackintosh joined Honeyman and Keppie as a draughtsman and for six years—until 1895, when MacNair left to set up his own practice—Mackintosh and MacNair worked in the same office. They went on sketching tours together, and a further bond between them (from about 1893) was their friendship with the Macdonald sisters, Margaret and Frances.

The interaction between these four artists was so intense that it is never easy to determine which one of them was the first to hit upon any particular idea. On the other hand, the known designs of MacNair have such stylistic peculiarities, or even obsessions, that it is possible to give him credit for the most interesting and most prophetic piece of early Glasgow-style furniture. It is the oak cabinet signed and dated 1895 and made, presumably, for his new studio in West George Street. It might even be the first of its kind, since Mackintosh's Guthrie & Wells furniture cannot be allocated to any certain date before 1896. Besides, whereas Mackintosh's furniture at this time is strongly Voysey-influenced, in spite of the distinctively Glasgow metal work on the linen press and the stencilled upholstery on the settle, MacNair's cabinet is more radical, purely functional in shape and at the same time utterly personal in decoration. The stylised swooping bird in the metal work below the cornice occurs again and again in his designs. The melancholy pierced-metal faces associated with the handles on the side doors (which open to facilitate the storing of long rolls of paper) appears also in the Glasgow Institute poster, on which MacNair collaborated with Margaret and Frances Macdonald in 1896.

The extension and abstraction of the swooping bird motif into the curving outlines of MacNair's remarkable smoker's cabinet might just have been inspired by the modelling over the doorway to Mackintosh's Marty's Public School (1896). However that may be, the smoker's cabinet, illustrated in the *Studio* in September, 1897, and obviously designed earlier, is the most imaginative piece of furniture either of them had made up to that time. It is equalled only by Mackintosh's famous chair with high back and oval head rest, designed for the Argyle Street tea rooms in 1897 but apparently not made until two or three years later. Although MacNair certainly could not compete with Mackintosh as an architect, he was not far behind him in poster design, and in furniture design he briefly led the way at a crucial point in the development of the Glasgow style.

An examination of photographs of MacNair's flat in Oxford Street, Liverpool, furnished in 1899 after his marriage to Frances Macdonald, and of Mackintosh's flat in Mains Street, Glasgow, furnished in 1900 after his marriage to Margaret Macdonald, shows how much more sophisticated Mackintosh's furniture had become. MacNair's seems clumsy in comparison. Clearly, Herbert and Frances made a special effort for their writing room in the Scottish section of the Turin Exhibition in 1902 and offered some interesting and successful exhibits, like the writing table with the inlaid panels on the broad stretchers, the glass-topped display tables on long and slender legs, and the revolving bookcase which seems to have inspired a similar piece of furniture in Mackintosh's music room at Hous'hill.

Sadly little or nothing survives of the group of objets d'art exhibited by the MacNairs in one of their display tables. It presumably included the jewellery they had shown at the Education Exhibition in Liverpool in 1901 and perhaps even some of the glass and metal ware from the same exhibition. Although there are other possible candidates, the only undisputed surviving examples of Herbert and Frances's silver work are the tea caddy and spoon made (and hallmarked) in 1897 as a wedding present for one of MacNair's sisters and the sugar tongs, another wedding present, for Mary 'Bee' Phillips. Both of these, like the one (partially) surviving item of table glass, are delightful and demonstrate how successful the MacNairs were when working on a small scale.

Even MacNair's failures have something likeable about them. The three-legged chair in the Turin writing room, with its minimal back rest, central front support and elongated seat, is an indication of his continued willingness to experiment and find new forms. As Mackintosh observed, 'There is hope in honest error . . .' MacNair's career was, however, a sad one, dogged by misfortune. It could even be argued that the private income which sustained him only until its withdrawal let him down in Liverpool was the worst misfortune of all. Addiction to drink—an even more serious problem for him than for Mackintosh—was certainly another.

The first actual disaster was the fire which destroyed much of his early work, including a whole series of stained glass designs, shortly before the *Studio* interviewed him in 1897. As a teacher—Instructor of Design in the School of Architecture and Applied Art in the University College of Liverpool—he was happy, well liked and successful. The MacNair flat was famous in Liverpool for its lead-lined hall and staircase, its (in Augustus John's words) 'multitude of spooks', and its 'very creepy' drawing room. Herbert and, presumably, Frances, who is unlikely to have remained inactive in spite of having a baby to look after, even inspired some of the younger designers to work in a style quite alien to Liverpool. There were probably not enough of them to make a Glasgow colony there, but Cassandia Ann Walker, a MacNair pupil and one of the most talented of the artists employed by the Della Robbia pottery in Birkenhead, decorated several vases in a quite unmistakable Glasgow manner. Phoebe McLeish, another MacNair pupil and one of several talented sisters, won an honourable mention in a *Studio* competition in 1902, evidently after being recommended to study Hornel and Jessie M. King, and three years later she was commended by the *Studio*'s Liverpool correspondent for a group of decorative work clearly influenced by the MacNairs. However, in 1905 the University closed down its art school and MacNair was out of a job. He and Frances stayed on for three more years, both teaching at the School of the Sandon Studios Society, and, when Herbert's private income ran out, returned to Glasgow.

If decorative commissions in Liverpool had been few—no more than two interiors, two medals, a poster for the Liverpool Academy, and a mere handful of other graphic designs—they were fewer still in Glasgow. In fact, nothing is known of any work MacNair did after his return to

Glasgow apart from the occasional watercolour, which he exhibited at the Sandon Studios Society and at the Baillie Gallery in London in 1911 and 1912. There are two possible explanations for this: either he did nothing else or everything has been lost. It is known that after Frances died in 1921 (according to the coroner's report from a cerebral haemorrhage) he vowed never to paint again. Even before that he must have been severely discouraged, not least by the Macdonald family's attempt to ship him off, alone, to Canada, and by having to work as a postman and to take other odd jobs while Frances was teaching in the School of Art. It is also known that in 1943, after the death of the sister with whom he was living in Argyll and before he moved into the old people's home where he died twelve years later, he destroyed a trunkful of his own and Frances's drawings. Some of them were saved, including a fascinating symbolist watercolour—dated as early as 1893—depicting an elongated male figure apparently entwined with the girl in the East wind in Frances's *Ill Omen* of the same year.

MacNair's devotion to Frances must have been unusually intense. Most of the figures in his graphic work seem to be based on her and she appears in several of his watercolours, including *Love in a Mist* of 1906 where she is bound in a kind of vegetable embrace with Herbert and their young son Sylvan. If the female figure in the designs becomes plumper and more conventional in time, this is not out of keeping with reality. It is noticeable, too, how in at least the watercolours he adopted her style at a very early stage. Where unsigned drawings and even metalwork and jewellery are concerned, definite attribution to one or the other is very difficult. Frances's imagery is usually more precise, however, and her draughtsmanship more skilful.

MARGARET AND FRANCES MACDONALD

The Macdonald sisters, whose family had moved to Glasgow from Staffordshire in the late 1880s, started attending drawing classes at the School of Art in 1891. Margaret was twenty-six at the time and Frances was seventeen. It is another indication of the favourable climate for a flowering of the decorative arts in Glasgow at the time—even without Mackintosh—that as soon as they left the school in 1894 Margaret and Frances opened a studio in Hope Street where they made and sold their metalwork and gesso panels, their embroideries and their jewellery. It is significant, too, that it was because their work had so much in common with that of Mackintosh and MacNair that the headmaster of the School, Fra Newbery, brought the four together: the young men being evening students and the girls being day students, they had never met before. It is not known exactly when the introduction took place but it was probably at some time in 1893, the year in which Mackintosh and MacNair left the School of Art. It is unlikely that the sisters would have developed an individual style before then, and it was in April 1893 that the first number of the *Studio* appeared with its influential reproductions of drawings by Aubrey Beardsley, who also designed the original cover for the magazine. And it was in 1893, in June, that J. M. Dent published the first part of Malory's *Le Morte d'Arthur* with covers and illustrations by Beardsley; in September of the same year the *Studio* published its evidently revelatory reproduction of Jan Toorop's *Three Brides*.

The availability of the Toorop reproduction and the Beardsley illustrations is stressed because it must have been some common inspiration which brought about such a noticeable similarity in the work of four students who had never met. There can be no doubt that all of them were influenced by these artists, Mackintosh no less than the others—although the more substantial background figure of Burne Jones should never be forgotten in this kind of context. Mackintosh's 1895 poster for the Glasgow Institute of the Fine Arts is clearly influenced by Beardsley; his 1893 design for the Diploma awarded by the Glasgow School of Art Club (the earliest known example of Glasgow art nouveau) derives both its composition and some of its details from the Toorop painting. On the other hand, the diploma also includes some very personal motifs, above all the espalier apple trees which grow from disproportionately large seeds in the lower corners to form both a framework and a background of branching right angles, each shoot terminating in a large single leaf, flower, or fruit. The framework of right-angled branches, with or without the seed and in more or less geometric abstraction, became one of the most common features of Glasgow-style design. Margaret and Frances adopted it immediately for both watercolours and metalwork, and MacNair used it in his bookplates and posters. It seems to have been Frances however who invented one of the most potent images, the flight of birds which swoops through so many Glasgow designs in pursuit of the ravens crossing the moon in her *Ill Omen*. Although it was not reproduced in the *Yellow Book* until 1896, *Ill Omen* is actually dated 1893. With its slender uprights enclosing a suspended disc and crossed by strong horizontals, it exemplifies much of the Glasgow style at a very early date. There is similar imagery in Mackintosh's 1892 watercolour *The Harvest Moon*, where the lunar disc is crossed by horizontal wisps of cloud, but the Walter Crane angel in the centre is a strangely alien feature. Although it was Mackintosh who invested the birds in *Ill Omen* with the kinetic energy they display in his 1894 Conversazione programme and in a later jewellery design, and although both Mackintosh and MacNair were fascinated by other aspects of birds in flight, it seems to have been Frances who first found such symbolic significance in them.

In *Ill Omen* there is a hint of the expressionist anxiety which, in later years, distinguishes Frances's work from that of her sister. In the mid 1890s there was no marked difference between them. Obviously, coming from the same background and sharing the same religious convictions—which provided them with an iconography more reverberant than anything in Beardsley—they were bound to see things in the same way. They frequently collaborated on the same projects—sometimes with Herbert MacNair as well—and when they worked independently they apparently had no objection to a joint attribution. If it is possible to make a distinction between them it could be that Frances was the more original, the more likely to create a new image, while Margaret had the more compelling decorative vision and the more developed sense of style. Mackintosh is reported as having said: 'Margaret has genius; I have only talent.' It was tribute enough that he did some water-colours very much in her style in the late 1890s, and that her two-dimensional work was an integral part of so many of his designs. It is remarkable with what flair she adapted her style as her husband's developed and as fashion changed. Her panels for the card room at Hous'hill in 1900, her menu for Miss Cranston's White Cockade tea rooms at the Glasgow Exhibition of 1911, and her fabric designs of the early 1920s are as assured and as stylish in their way as her art nouveau compositions in the 1890s.

FRA NEWBERY Fra Newbery's introduction of the Macdonald sisters to Mackintosh and MacNair was significant not only because of its consequences and not only because of the implication that Margaret and Frances had independently produced distinctive decorative work. It indicates also how perceptive Newbery was and what interest he took both in his students and in the decorative arts. In fact, in 1893, the year when the introduction most likely took place, he organised a series of lectures at the School of Art on the arts and crafts. Without his influence, above all in making sure that Mackintosh's design won the competition for the new School of Art, the Glasgow style would certainly not have developed as it did. Equally, even without Mackintosh, he would have encouraged whatever talent there was in Glasgow for the arts and crafts.

In 1885, when he came from London to take up his new appointment in Glasgow, Newbery was still only thirty-one and not too old to enjoy the friendship of his students. In 1889 he married one of them, Jessie Rowat, daughter of a manufacturer of Paisley shawls, and she, as Jessie Newbery, became one of the most imaginative of British embroidery designers. In London, as a teacher at the South Kensington Schools and an admirer of William Morris, Newbery was in touch with the English arts and crafts movement, and in Glasgow he was in a unique position to encourage the establishment of a Scottish equivalent. It is another mark of his perception in this area that when the memorial stone of the new School of Art was laid in 1898 it contained an illuminated history of the school by Jessie M. King, who was then a student of twenty-two. E. A. Taylor, Jessie King's future husband and an influential commercial designer, also studied at the School. By 1902, when Newbery organised the Scottish section at the International Exhibition of Decorative Art at Turin, he was able to include examples of the work not only of the Mackintoshes, the MacNairs, Jessie Newbery, Jessie King and E. A. Taylor but also of students and recent students such as Ann Macbeth, Agnes Harvey, de Courcy Dewar, P. Wylie Davidson and Jessie Keppie (sister of John Keppie, of Honeyman & Keppie, and a former fiancée of Charles Rennie Mackintosh).

TALWIN MORRIS In the section devoted to the second generation of Glasgow stylists at Turin there were several exhibits by a designer who, because of his maturity and his long standing friendship with the Four, belongs in a sense to the first generation and could almost be counted a fifth member of what the *Studio* called the 'Mac group'. Talwin Morris was not an original artist but he was the first collector of work by the Four and the first to translate their ideas into commercial and multiple terms. Born in Winchester in 1865, Morris came to Glasgow in May, 1893—a crucial month in the development of the style—to take up his post of art director in Blackie's publishing house. His interest in the Mac group is demonstrated by his acquisition of some of the earliest examples of their decorative work, like the Mackintosh settle which aroused such indignation at the Arts and Crafts exhibition in London in 1896, the peacock wall sconce by Margaret and Frances Macdonald, and Frances's monumental pair of beaten brass candlesticks.

The most interesting of Morris's own craftwork, some of which was illustrated in a *Studio* article on Glasgow designers in 1897, is in beaten metal. Much of it was done for his home at Dunglass Castle, a house which he later sold to the parents of the Macdonald sisters and which was then redecorated by Mackintosh. There were some exquisitely wrought metal door handles, finger plates and panels, sometimes based on his own feline obsession but in unmistakably Mac-derived style, as well as stencilled decorations. Although he had trained as an architect he did not excel in three-dimensional design and few examples of his furniture are known. A metal-mounted bookcase was illustrated in the *Studio* in October, 1900, and there is a wardrobe at present on view in the Glasgow Art Gallery. Nor are there many known survivors of his fascinating buckles and brooches in beaten silver, copper and even aluminium illustrated in *Modern Design in Jewellery and Fans* in about 1900. There are, on the other hand, countless examples of the book covers he designed for Blackie. The rose motif, derived by the Glasgow artists from Beardsley, is in profuse abundance, often in association with the espalier branches and, in one particularly attractive design, with the singing birds in Mackintosh's poster for the *Scottish Musical Review*. Most of the Glasgow-style motifs find their way on to the Blackie covers where, although they frequently have no relevance to the contents of the book and lose their symbolic significance, their decorative potential is skilfully exploited. If Morris had done nothing else, incidentally, his influence in securing for Mackintosh the commission for a new home for the Blackie family—the Hill House at Helensburgh—would be conclusive proof of his good taste.

JESSIE M. KING
Among the book covers exhibited in the Scottish section at Turin, the most successful—in that it won its designer a gold medal—was not by Talwin Morris but by Jessie M. King. At this time she was instructor in book decoration at the School of Art and one of the most accomplished of decorative artists working in Glasgow. Her illustrations had been attracting attention since her student days and *Studio* reproductions of her early work show how quickly she had found her distinctive style. Only a few months after her awkward mixture of oriental and Glasgow imagery in an illustration for *The Light of Asia* (June, 1898) she achieved a far more convincing and, as it turned out, thoroughly characteristic blend of imagery in the mixed fairy-tale and art nouveau inspiration of her illustrations for *Wynken, Blynken and Nod* (January, 1899).

Jessie King was never a pure Glasgow stylist. Her child-like vision and the proliferation of line and decorative detail, although exquisitely realised, separate her work from the comparatively simple, symbolically reverberant designs of the Four at their best. In her graphic work she came nearest to them round about 1900–1902, when she designed for

William Rowat an economically drawn bookplate with something of the mystic content of Four work and an atmospheric watercolour panel for a sensational screen by George Logan. However, she proved to be adaptable, versatile and popular. She had the longest career of any of the Glasgow decorative artists, extending from about 1898 until her death in 1949. She was, moreover, the only one who continued to win both applause and commissions from London without settling permanently in England. Her main activity was with books. She was involved with more than a hundred of them—as cover designer, illustrator, compiler and even writer—for many different Scottish, English and continental publishers. But she was also prolific in other kinds of decorative work, like wallpapers for the Glasgow furnishers Wylie & Lochhead, textiles for Alexander Morton & Co., and a variety of things for Liberty of London. Apart from George Walton, who no longer lived in Scotland, she was the only Glasgow artist to be represented in the international bazaar of art nouveau in Regent Street. To judge by the large number of designs in her style in the Liberty records, she was one of the most successful of Liberty's jewellery designers (second only to Archibald Knox, who was responsible for more than anyone else). There are several gold necklaces incorporating wirework roses, like the one illustrated in the 1909 *Studio Year-Book of eDcorative Art*, a number of interesting gold pendants, and some particularly attractive silver and enamel buttons, brooches, and buckles decorated with the elliptical curves, roses and flying birds familiar from the work of the Four. Jessie King's jewellery designs are among the best of all commercial adaptations of the Glasgow style and they remained in the Liberty catalogues from about 1905 for twenty years or more, until long after the style (and Glasgow) had been abandoned by its major protagonists.

How Jessie King might have developed without the Mackintosh and Macdonald inspiration it is not impossible to imagine. A gift like hers, carefully and understandingly fostered by Newbery, would not have remained hidden. The Burne Jones and Beardsley influences, her keen observation of minute detail, her exceptionally fine linear ability, and her child-like imagination would possibly have combined to create an artist not very different from the Jessie King we know. Moreover, like Margaret Macdonald and unlike some of their Glasgow contemporaries, she was not so limited that, when the prevailing taste turned from art nouveau mannerism, she was left stranded with an obsolete idiom and no one to communicate with. It is true that she retained her early style for a surprisingly long time, though probably not as long as is suggested by the appearance of the set of *Seven Happy Days* in the 1913 Christmas Number of the *Studio*. These almost certainly date from several years earlier, and at least one of them was exhibited in 1909. In 1913 she had been living in Paris for two years, drawing bridges, buildings and monuments to add to her decorative characterisations of similar subjects in Culross, Edinburgh and Glasgow. The line had already thickened by this time and, although the fairy-tale figures continue to appear in her illustrations and covers, they are now composed of bold patches of colour, almost as if they were stencilled on to the page. Bakst has been suggested by Cordelia Oliver as one influence on her changing style and her interest in batik dyeing as another.

When the outbreak of war sent Jessie King and her husband back to Scotland they settled not in Glasgow but in Kirkcudbright, on the Solway coast, where they established a new style. The Kirkcudbright style is obviously descended from Glasgow, a deliberately naive, whimsical version epitomised by the witty nursery she exhibited at the Exposition de l'Art pour L'Enfance at the Musée Galliéra in 1912. In interior and furniture design this was her level. The Kirkcudbright style is innocent of all symbolism and any meaning beneath the simple shapes and bright colours on the surface. It lent itself well to fabric and dress designs, some of them in batik, and to painting on pottery. Although Jessie King did throw her own at one time, the pottery which she decorated at Kirkcudbright during the last thirty years of her life was brought either from large factories like Mintons or from local kilns. She usually painted on the biscuit body which was then sent away for glazing. Although most of these pieces are quite unambitious—some of them scarcely more than tourist wares to be sold at the Paul Jones Cafe in Kirkcudbright—they are all very charming, each one in its own way. When Jessie King died in 1949, leaving behind a number of unfired ceramic decorations, the Glasgow style died with her.

WYLIE & LOCHHEAD E. A. Taylor survived his wife by three years. He, however, had long since given up decorative work and, apart from designing a few book covers and making the occasional contribution to the stock of painted pottery at the Paul Jones Cafe, had devoted most of his time in Kirkcudbright to landscape painting and teaching. As a designer, he had achieved his greatest distinction exactly fifty years before his death at the Turin Exhibition of 1902, where he was represented by two stained-glass panels, two cabinets, a screen and a small table. They are excellent examples of Taylor's very successful combination of Scottish and

English features. The birds in the stained-glass panel designed for a wardrobe, though related to the early Glasgow-style ravens and swallows, have more in common with the plump Baillie Scott species. The table and the cabinets, though innocent of commercial marquetry and decorated instead with little glass panels of Glasgow roses, are supported on the long and slender legs characteristic of English art nouveau and even Edwardian design.

Most of E. A. Taylor's furniture, including his Turin exhibits, was designed for and made by the Glasgow firm of Wylie & Lochhead. It is this basic fact which distinguishes his decorative work from that of the Four. He and his colleagues at Wylie and Lochhead, George Logan and John Ednie, were designing furniture which was intended to make a general appeal and to fit into the middle-class home. With Wylie & Lochhead bedroom suites costing up to £250, which was a lot of money by Edwardian standards, it would have been cheaper to commission an exclusive design from Charles Rennie Mackintosh, but only the most enlightened patrons were prepared to live under the strict regime of a Mackintosh interior. The Glasgow public went to the store in Buchanan Street for the compromise they wanted and found there a range of modern furniture of a style and quality unequalled by any comparable commercial enterprise in Europe.

How long Wylie & Lochhead were supplying Glasgow-style furniture it is difficult to say. Their furnishing catalogues from around the turn of the century are hard to come by, and those which are available are not dated. The self-congratulatory booklet produced by the firm on its 125th anniversary in 1954 makes no mention of this most distinguished period in its history. It is unlikely however that it lasted for more than seven years. Certainly, the first occasion which brought the name of Wylie & Lochhead to the attention of the readers of the *Studio* was the Glasgow Exhibition of 1901. Being cabinet makers to Queen Victoria and having furnished the royal suite at the Glasgow Exhibition of 1888, it was a matter of course that they should undertake a similar responsibility in 1901 (as they did also in 1911, 1938 and 1951). It is still more to the credit of Wylie & Lochhead that in 1901, as well as supplying the traditional furnishings for the royal reception rooms, they built a pavilion in the Glasgow style with rooms designed by E. A. Taylor, George Logan and John Ednie. According to Hermann Muthesius, who reviewed the event for *Dekorative Kunst*, this was the first British exhibition to present completely furnished rooms as examples of the designer's art. He was most impressed by the Wylie & Lochhead pavilion, in spite of competition from George Walton, Ambrose Heal and Henri Van de Velde,* as well as other arts and crafts furnishers in Glasgow, like A. Gardner of Jamaica Street and Francis Smith of St Vincent Street.

It is interesting too that Muthesius gives Taylor the credit for all four of the rooms. This was obviously a misunderstanding, since the *Studio* account of the exhibition clearly attributes the dining room to Ednie, the bedroom to Logan, and only the drawing room to Taylor (the library is not specifically attributed, but it is in fact the same room as the library illustrated in the *Studio* article on George Logan in December 1903). Muthesius's error might however help to solve a problem—which is that very few items of Wylie & Lochhead furniture are definitely and wholly attributable to any one designer: not even those which appear in contemporary illustrations with a designer's name attached can be accepted as his work in every detail. A vivid example of the confusion is the chair which is illustrated in one issue of the *Studio* as the work of E. A. Taylor and which reappears in another above the name of George Logan. The likely explanation, following Muthesius's hint, is that Taylor was the chief designer in Wylie & Lochhead's art furniture department and that he was responsible for maintaining a house style. The advantages of this would have been that glass panels, say, or metal hinges and handles designed by Taylor could be applied without too much incongruity to the furniture of Logan or Ednie and that an interior decoration scheme undertaken by one of them could include items designed by the others.

On the other hand, it is possible to associate certain characteristics with each designer. Taylor, for example, derived less from Mackintosh than did the other two. This was not because he admired Mackintosh less but, presumably, because his ideas as a designer had been formed to some extent before he came under Mackintosh's influence. He had trained first as a draughtsman in a Clyde shipyard and he was already well into his twenties when, in the late 1890s, he became a student at the Glasgow School of Art. Inevitably, working in a Mackintosh milieu, he absorbed some of its features, but not so much the architectural fundamentals as the decorative motifs—the stylised rose which reappears in his stained glass and metal panels and, among others, the elegantly split heart pierced in the corners of his furniture. Moreover, he seems to have had a wider interest in contemporary design in general. As the *Studio* said of his drawing room in the 1901 exhibition, he had evidently made 'a careful study of the best modern designers'. It was a double-edged

* Although Muthesius mentions a shop interior by Van de Velde in his report of the exhibition the minutely detailed Official Catalogue does not confirm its presence.

comment but it did him no harm since the commissions for the interiors in the Coats house in Birmingham, Lord Weir's house in Glasgow, and the King's Head Hotel in Sheffield came to him soon after exhibition.

John Ednie was much more the Mackintosh disciple. Though he was educated at the Edinburgh School of Art, he came to Glasgow, according to the *Studio*, 'early in the history of the "modern renaissance" and from the beginning was strongly identified with it'. The first public display of his work was at the Glasgow Exhibition in 1901, where he was responsible not only for the dining room in the Wylie & Lochhead pavilion but also for a tea-room interior. The watercolour designs for both these rooms were exhibited in the Scottish section at Turin in 1902 and they still survive although, following a mistake (one of several) in Alexander Koch's Turin review, they are traditionally attributed to a certain Jane Fonie (and were catalogued as such in Sotheby's sale of the contents of Jessie M. King's and E. A. Taylor's studio in 1977). In Vittorio Pica's account of the Turin Exhibition they are attributed to John Edwie, which is obviously a misprint for John Ednie and which makes more sense. The 'little known' Jane Fonie never existed, like George Ednie and John Edine, who have also been credited with work done by John Ednie. This confusion is unfortunate since it has been an obstacle to a clear view of an exceptionally stylish designer. Like Taylor, he was influenced by Baillie Scott—whose furniture was another line sold by Wylie & Lochhead—but the main source of his inspiration was Mackintosh. He was the only one of these three Wylie & Lochhead designers whose furniture has anything like the sculptural interest of Mackintosh's. Shallow carving, of butterfly and leaf motifs, is common in the work of all three of them, but the elaborate combinations of *cyma recta* and *inversa* cornices and the curving and tapering convex mouldings reliably identify the hand of John Ednie. He designed flat surfaces too, of course, and he often decorated them with the squares and chequers which Taylor and Logan usually avoided. But, having been trained as an architect—which Taylor and, one imagines, Logan were not—Ednie is most distinctive in three dimensions. His chairs, for example, have a particularly interesting and attractive structural character.

As for George Logan, his most distinctive work is his fanciful watercolour interiors rather than the actual furniture which is known to have been made to his design. Indeed, some of his ideas are so unrealistic that one sometimes wonders whether he was not a figment of the combined imaginations of E. A. Taylor and Jessie M. King. The presence of a Logan watercolour in the contents of the Taylors' studio (attributed by

Sotheby's to Jessie M. King), together with a mixture of unsigned Logan and Taylor designs in a private collection which derives from the same source, would seem to lend some substance to the theory. However, if Taylor was the chief designer for this particular Wylie & Lochhead department, it is not unlikely that both Ednie and Logan designs would have come into his possession and that he would have retained them. Besides, there is something depressingly realistic about the solidly furnished dining room illustrated in the *Studio* as the work of George Logan in an article on him in December 1903. The same article reproduces some his watercolour interiors, which are obviously overcrowded with decorative detail but which include some imaginative light fittings, stylish carpets and delightfully elegant chairs and tables. The chairs obviously derive from Mackintosh in shape if not in their gothic elaboration but, if ever they were made, they seem to have disappeared without trace. One piece in Logan's fanciful manner which was made, however, and which has (for the most part) survived is the remarkable screen which he designed for the Scottish section of the Turin Exhibition. One very fascinating feature, which again seems to lend substance to suspicions about the origins of George Logan, is Jessie M. King's *Princesses of the Red Rose* in the central panel. This drawing, representing the artist at her best, the carving on the wooden frame, and the characteristic abstract patterns in applied silver on the side panels, though overfussy in detail, make the screen one of the most attractive of all examples of the Glasgow style. Between the solid and the fanciful, there is a third kind of Logan design, unmistakably in the Wylie & Lochhead house style but with more than the usual proportion of inlaid and shallow-carved decoration. The 1903 *Studio* article illustrates two such rooms which he designed for the Glasgow Exhibition in 1901—a bedroom in walnut and a library in mahogany (the latter including a monumental bookcase which was once in the Handley Read collection and which is now stored out of sight in the Victoria and Albert Museum).

Until further information comes to light it is impossible to estimate how productive Logan was as a designer. It is almost certain that he supplied Foley and other Staffordshire potteries with some stylish decorations and he certainly designed metalwork for Wylie & Lochhead. But even less is known about him than about John Ednie. We have little more biographical information about him than that he exhibited six times at the Glasgow Institute of the Fine Arts (presumably watercolours) between 1898 and 1904 and that he lived at 17 Ardgowan Street, Greenock—the address inscribed on his watercolour interior, *The White*

Boudoir, reproduced in the *Studio* in November 1905 to illustrate his own rhapsodic article, *A Colour Symphony*. Here, in a synaesthetic fanfare, George Logan leaves the scene. Apart from a desperately nostalgic circa 1902 interior design reproduced in the *Studio Year Book* for 1912, the last heard of John Ednie was the announcement in 1908 of his appointment as art superintendent at the Glasgow and West of Scotland Technical College (where E. A. Taylor had taught before him). It was also in 1908 that Taylor married Jessie King and left Glasgow for Manchester to become designer-manager of George Wragge Ltd., specialists in stained glass. Three years later they moved to Paris, and Taylor had almost abandoned design in favour of painting and teaching.

THE CRISIS Obviously, by 1908 there was little demand in Glasgow for Glasgow-style design. Mackintosh was as much hurt by the change of taste as anyone—perhaps even more than anyone except MacNair, whose decision to return home and seek refuge in Glasgow in 1908 was singularly ill-timed. It is sad to think of the celebrated Four sitting together amid suddenly outmoded furniture in the Mackintosh home in Southpark Avenue awaiting commissions and consoling themselves for their non-arrival with drink. Mackintosh was at this time not so much 'in decline' (as Howarth bluntly puts it) as passing through a severe artistic crisis. He spent, in fact, six years looking for a new style, as the Cloister and Chinese Rooms in Ingram Street clearly suggest, and failing to find one, although even at this stage he seemed to be moving towards the continental Secessionist style which was to have such an influence on the interiors of 78 Derngate in 1916. The gravestone which Mackintosh designed for Talwin Morris in 1911, and which would not have looked at all out of place in Vienna or Darmstadt, is a melancholy memorial to the Glasgow style.

Had Glasgow sustained its interest in the contemporary decorative arts, had Mackintosh been able to sustain the elation which he felt when at work on such late tea-room projects as the Cloister and Chinese Rooms, he would surely have survived the crisis. He would have developed his ideas on new and yet distinctively personal lines, perhaps moving further towards the simplicity characteristic of the best design in the years round the First World War. But Glasgow let him down. Whereas, as we have seen, it was a fertile ground for the decorative arts in the early 1890s—even without a seminal genius like Mackintosh—fifteen years later it was a far from encouraging environment for an adventurous designer. Indeed, by 1914 it was so inimical to Mackintosh that he retired to Walberswick to join the Newberys and draw wild flowers. Having escaped from his crisis in this way, but not having surmounted it, when called upon to find a style for his next (and last) major decorative project at 78 Derngate, Northampton, he turned to the Viennese Secession, the design principles of which he had himself helped to form.

So, while Vienna flourished, Glasgow decayed. The major protagonists of the Glasgow style had left, had died, or had been defeated by apathy. Wylie & Lochhead no longer had any use for Taylor, Logan and Ednie. Miss Cranston retained her faith in the commercial value of Mackintosh's designs, but the growth of her tea room business was interrupted by the war and, after the death of her husband in 1917, she lost all interest in it. In the years just before and after the war the style survived in Glasgow only on the two-dimensional level, in the embroideries of the pupils of Jessie Newbery and Ann Macbeth, in Oscar Paterson's stained glass studios, in the countless beaten metal mirror frames and wall sconces of craftsmen and women like Margaret Gilmour and Mary R. Henderson, in the hand-painted pottery of Jessie Keppie and Elizabeth Mary Watts, and in the decorative watercolours of such lady artists as Annie French, Cecile Walton and Meg Wright. Much of this work is stylistically debased and not very interesting, although occasionally, given a fresh impetus, something striking would emerge. And in Kirkcudbright the indefatigable Jessie King retained the freshness of her decorative vision in spite of all the odds against it.

Although the initiative in progressive design had by 1910 passed to Austria and Germany, in the fifteen or so years round the turn of the century Scotland had created a decorative style distinguished by an emotional fervour associated normally only with painting and sculpture. Whatever the Secessionist designers and architects had learned from Mackintosh, that quality is only rarely found in their work—in one or two pieces of jewellery by Kolo Moser and Otto Prutscher, in some of Josef Hoffmann's furniture and metalwork, and in the best ceramic designs of Henri Van de Velde. In England it is occasionally to be found in the silver and jewellery of Archibald Knox; in France in the early work of Rene Lalique; in Holland in J. Juriaan Kok's designs for Rozenburg pottery—which is to say, in the most inspired work of some of the most gifted of European designers. In Glasgow, for a few years, the creative excitement penetrated below that level, to artists who, in another place at another time, would have produced nothing worth preserving. What inspired them, and sustained them for a dozen or so precious years, was their delight in a style which they not only absorbed from the light shed by Charles Rennie Mackintosh, but which they also drew in as a natural process from their Glasgow roots.

BIBLIOGRAPHY

The best source of information on the arts and crafts in England and Scotland is still *The Studio* magazine, in spite of its occasional inaccuracies and contradictions. Beginning in April 1893, the early issues actually influenced the formation of the Glasgow style and later numbers, generously if inconsistently, recorded its development and decline. Several other *Studio* publications—*Modern British Domestic Architecture and Decoration* (1901), *Modern Design in Jewellery and Fans* (1901–2), and the *Yearbooks of Decorative Art* (from 1906)—are also essential reading. A similar compilation, *The British Home of Today*, edited by Walter Shaw Sparrow and published by Hodder & Stoughton (London 1905) is valuable for its illustrations of interiors by George Walton. As for contemporary periodicals apart from *The Studio*, the English ones like *The Artist* and *The Art Journal* have proved less fruitful than the German ones like *Dekorative Kunst* and *Deutsche Kunst und Dekoration*. However, all the relevant contemporary documents repay study—the professional magazines like *Academy Architecture* and the *Architectural Review*, trade catalogues like those issued by Wylie & Lochhead and Liberty, and exhibition catalogues and reports, such as those for Glasgow in 1901 and Turin in 1902 (Vittorio Pica's *L'Arte decorativa all'Espozione di Torino del 1902* is recommended in preference to Alexander Koch's misleading account of the same exhibition). A vivid impression of the Scottish East-coast style is given by the four numbers of *The Evergreen* published in Edinburgh and London by Patrick Geddes between 1895 and 1897.

Of the modern writers who have concerned themselves with the Glasgow style, Thomas Howarth made the outstanding contribution in his *Charles Rennie Mackintosh and the Modern Movement*, first published in London in 1952. It is a pity that he could not take the opportunity to carry out a thorough revision in the second edition (1977) but the book is still the most comprehensive account of Mackintosh's life and work, and there is in it the basis for a study of the Glasgow style in general. Robert Macleod's *Charles Rennie Mackintosh* (London 1968) looks at the architect from a different point of view, and a useful supplement to Howarth and Macleod is provided by Andrew McLaren Young's catalogue (recently reprinted) for the Mackintosh centenary exhibition at the Edinburgh Festival in 1968. Roger Billcliffe, McLaren Young's successor as the Glasgow authority on Mackintosh, has published two books on the graphic work, *Architectural Sketches & Flower Drawings by Charles Rennie Mackintosh* (London 1977) and, particularly valuable, *Mackintosh Watercolours* (London 1978). We await Billcliffe's complete catalogue of the Mackintosh furniture and interiors with great interest and, in the meantime, acknowledge our debt to his early work on MacNair, *J. H. MacNair in Glasgow and Liverpool,* published in the *Annual Report and Bulletin of the Walker Art Gallery, Liverpool, 1970–71.* Roger Billcliffe is also joint author (with Peter Vergo) of an article on *Charles Rennie Mackintosh and the Austrian Art Revival,* which was published in the *Burlington Magazine* in November 1977. There is an earlier article on *Mackintosh and Vienna* by Eduard F. Sekler reprinted in *The Anti-Rationalists* (London 1973) together with David Walker's *The Early Work of Charles Rennie Mackintosh.*

Although we have mentioned by no means all the Mackintosh material—and we should certainly add Filipo Alison: *Charles Rennie Mackintosh as a Designer of Chairs* (Milan and New York 1973); H. Jefferson Barnes: *Charles Rennie Mackintosh Furniture* and *Charles Rennie Mackintosh Ironwork and Metalwork* (both 1968); Jackie Cooper: *Mackintosh Architecture* (London 1978); and Pamela Reekie's exhibition catalogue *Charles Rennie Mackintosh, the Chelsea Years* (1978)—we have to say that there is very little written about his Glasgow colleagues and contemporaries. Cordelia Oliver prepared a pioneering catalogue for a Jessie M. King exhibition organised by the Scottish Arts Council in 1971 and she, together with Joan Hughson and H. Jefferson Barnes, contributed articles to the catalogue of the sale of the contents of the Jessie M. King and E. A. Taylor studio in 1977. There are several errors of attribution in the sale catalogue (published jointly by Sotheby's Belgravia and Paul Harris) but it is a well illustrated and indispensable document. Nikolaus Pevsner, who was writing illuminatingly about Mackintosh as early as 1936 in his *Pioneers of the Modern Movement,* published an important article on George Walton in the *RIBA Journal* three years later (and reprinted it in his *Studies in Art, Architecture and Design* in 1968). Most of the information we have been able to supply on the other Glasgow designers outside the "Mac Group" has been gleaned from contemporary, i.e. turn of the century, sources.

With the Glasgow school of painters the situation is quite different of course. There are several authoritative works of reference and criticism in this case, beginning with Sir J. L. Caw's monumental *Scottish Painting Past and Present 1620–1908* (London 1908, reprinted 1975) and including William Hardie's *Scottish Painting 1837–1939* (London 1976) which we have found most useful from the point of view of the decorative arts.

The following selection of illustrations, from the Mackintosh entrance to the Jessie M. King exit, has been loosely organised in a room-by-room sequence—hall, dining room, library/study, games room, gallery, bedroom/nursery, boudoir. However, where it has seemed illuminating to introduce objects with no related function to those around them, like the memorial to Talwin Morris in the library and the exterior railing in the gallery, we have not hesitated to do so, incongruous though this might be from the formal point of view. Indeed, such juxtapositions are one of the main points of the book.

1. The way into the Glasgow Style can only be through a Mackintosh entrance. We could have chosen the famous stained glass door of the rooms de luxe in the Willow Tea Rooms, or the main entrance to the School of Art; a less familiar and more appropriate example is this, the doorway designed in 1908 for the Lady Artists' Club at 5 Blythswood Square, Glasgow. Mackintosh's grooved pilasters and Greek pediment are a witty commentary on the neo-classical facade of the building, while the architect's Glasgow individuality is retained in the squared windows at the sides and the carved detail at the top of the pilasters. There are similar pilasters, with modified Ionic capitals, in the boardroom of the School of Art. (*Photograph   Victor Albrow*)

2, 3. J. Gaff Gillespie's entrance hall at 12 University Gardens, Glasgow, shows the influence of Mackintosh in its pattern of rectangular glass panels in the door, although it was designed six years before Mackintosh's entrance to the Lady Artists' Club. The panels of stained glass, arranged in a pleasing asymmetry, are by Oscar Paterson. The staircase has something of the sombre Scottish Baronial character of Salmon and Gillespie's interiors, but the fitted settle is a good and stylish example of Scottish arts and crafts. (*Photograph   Victor Albrow*)

4. Mackintosh's remarkable abstract stencilled panel for the hall of Hill House. (*Photograph   Victor Albrow*)

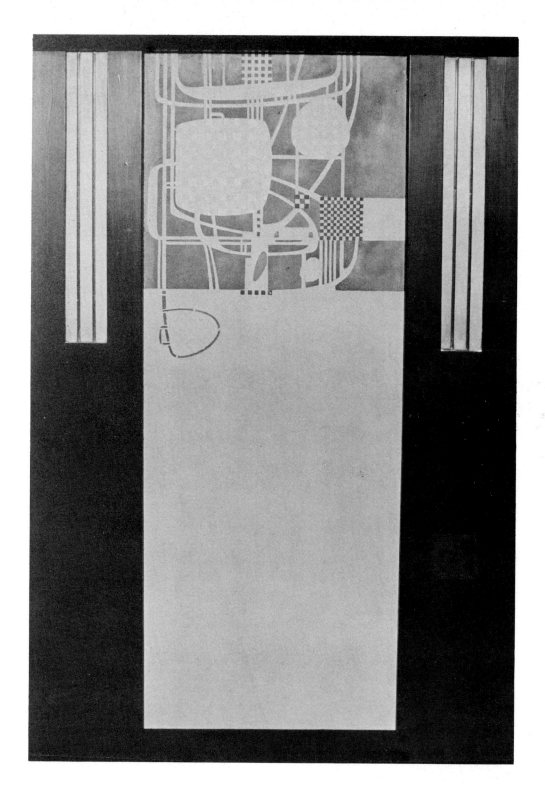

5. Lord Weir's house in Pollokshields, Glasgow, was completely refitted by the firm of Wylie and Lochhead in 1901–2. The designs are by E. A. Taylor whose discreetly luxurious oak panelling offsets the colourful exuberance of his stained glass. The bird motif on the windows and the roses on the door panels (both derived from Mackintosh) are very characteristic of the work of E. A. Taylor and his colleagues. (*Contemporary photograph*)

6, 7. Two examples of hall furniture designed by the English architect M. H. Baillie Scott, appearing in a Wylie and Lochhead catalogue of circa 1902. After Mackintosh, Baillie Scott was the strongest external influence on the Wylie and Lochhead designers.
(*Private collection.   Photograph   Victor Albrow*)

8. This oak hall chair combines so many Glasgow characteristics (in the pierced and curved apron below the seat, and in the cornice, and the triangular seat) with an apparently unmistakable Baillie Scott inlaid panel that it is difficult to attribute it to either with certainty.
(*Collection William McLean.*
Photograph Victor Albrow)

9. It would, on the other hand, be impossible to mistake the identity of this high-backed chair in stained beech, with its cubic construction incorporating floor-level stretchers, in spite of the fact that the gesso insert is a recent replacement of a lost original. The designer is unknown.
(*Private collection.   Photograph   Victor Albrow*)

10. A preliminary design, later modified, for the hall in the Haus eines Kunstfreundes. Mackintosh's entry for the competition organised by Alexander Koch of Darmstadt 1901. Although the house was never built the designs were published in Germany, where they had considerable influence on progressive architects. The delicate mural stencil, which does not appear in the final design, is the kind of decorative pattern which helped to form the style of Mackintosh's Glasgow contemporaries. (*University of Glasgow*)

11. A leaflet designed in 1907 by Jessie M. King for the Arcadian restaurant by Henry T. Wise, which was not in Miss Cranston's chain, but which obviously did cater for the artistic interests of the patrons of Glasgow tea-rooms. The pictorial content is pure Jessie King, but the decorative motifs associated with the lettering derive directly from Mackintosh— compare them with the stained glass door panels of the preceding illustration. (*Glasgow University*)

13. Mackintosh's design for a dining room, usually identified as being for an Austrian or German client.
(*Glasgow University*)

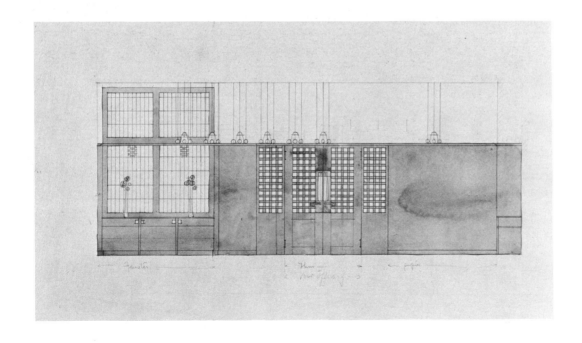

14. This contemporary photograph, which has not been published for seventy years or more, shows that the room was designed for an exhibition of interiors by A. S. Ball, Berlin in 1907. It is the only photograph that shows both chairs in full, and it is evident that the stained glass panel in the window was modified after the original design was made. The ceiling lights are less interesting than in the drawing. (*Photograph originally published by Ernst Wasmuth, Berlin*)

15. Mackintosh's clock for W. J. Bassett Lowke at 78 Derngate, Northampton, 1915–17, retains the squared trellis which by this time had become a convention of such English arts and crafts figures as Ambrose Heal and Ernest Gimson. The wooden latches derive from this tradition, and seem to show Mackintosh following, rather than leading, although the clock-face and the drawer-handles are distinctly modernist.
(*Victoria and Albert Museum*)

16. Another, more whimsical, use of the trellis in design, in a book wrapper by Jessie King, here supporting Glasgow roses.
(*Photograph Sotheby's*)

17. An imaginative use of the square, with domino dots to indicate the hours, in a clock designed by Mackintosh and executed in ebony and ivory by German prisoners of war on the Isle of Man. The construction, as a square flower growing from a multiple stem, is a geometric development of Mackintosh's earliest stylised plant designs.
(*Collection Mrs Sturrock.*
Photograph   Victor Albrow)

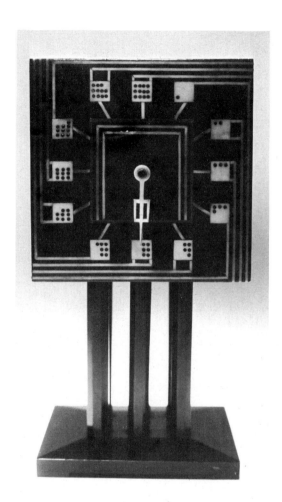

18. A Mackintosh chair incorporating both the cube and the square as structural and decorative basis.
(*Fine Art Society. Photograph Stephen Daniels*)

19. An example of the way in which the square was taken up by continental designers, in a wicker chair by H. Vollmer executed by the Viennese firm of Prag-Rudnicker. It is interesting that the Scottish element of this chair, which was reproduced in *The Studio* in 1904, so appealed to the artistic community in Glasgow that several copies were made for them by local craftsmen. One of these chairs, painted black, appeared in the sale of the studio contents of Jessie King and E. A. Taylor in 1977. Another is still owned by Mrs Sturrock, the daughter of Fra Newbery, the headmaster of the Glasgow School of Art from 1885.
(*Contemporary photograph*)

20. Two chairs from a dining room suite
which obviously derives from Mackintosh.
The designer is not known, but it is possible
that they were made by the same firm as that
which produced the chair in illustration no. 9.
(*Collection A. F. Armstrong.*
Photograph   James Morrison)

21. The chairs in a breakfast room designed by the Stockholm architect C. Westman are Scottish in style, as is the woodwork round the window bay. This room, like Mackintosh's no. 13, was designed for A. S. Ball's exhibition of interiors in Berlin. (*Contemporary photograph*)

22. A related chair by a Scottish designer, part of a Wylie and Lochhead bedroom suite, attributed to John Ednie.
(*Private collection.   Photograph   Victor Albrow*)

D

23. Argyle Street tearooms, *The Studio*, October 1906.

24. Henri van de Velde must have visited Glasgow or read *The Studio* before designing the armchairs in this photograph (1907). It is unlikely that they would have taken this form without the inspiration of the chairs in the luncheon room of Argyle Street. (*Contemporary photograph*)

25. This heavy oak chair, clearly based on the chairs in the luncheon room of the Argyle Street tearooms, might have been made as a replacement at some late date. There is a whole category of what might be called post-Mackintosh furniture, made loosely to his designs and not under his supervision. (*Private collection. Photograph Victor Albrow*)

26 is George Walton's adaptation of a traditional Scottish chair, used in Miss Cranston's Buchanan Street tearooms, 1896, and in Kodak showrooms in several European cities.
(*Fine Art Society.   Photograph   Stephen Daniels*)

27 (below) is Richard Riemerschmidt's version.
(*Museum Bellerive, Zurich*)

28 is by Alfred Althaus of Berlin.
(*Contemporary photograph*)

There is another very interesting British variant
in a room said to be designed and executed by
Goodyer's of Regent Street, illustrated in
The Studio Yearbook of Decorative Art, 1906,
page 26. All the Goodyer's interiors illustrated
in this yearbook were clearly designed either
by Walton or by a follower of his.

29. It is difficult to believe that Walton designed this elegant ebonised chair in Aesthetic style, at the same time as the arts and crafts ash one, or that it was used in the same tearoom and showrooms. It was the basis of numerous variants in Walton's interior decorative schemes for years afterwards, in spite of the obvious fragility of its slender out-turned front legs.
(*Fine Art Society. Photograph Stephen Daniels*)

30. Two ladderback dining chairs by Mackintosh, the first designed for the Willow tearooms in 1904, the second for 78 Derngate in 1916. The earlier chair, little more than traditional at first sight, is a classic of understated sculptural perfection.
(*Fine Art Society. Photograph Stephen Daniels*)

31. (Below) The later one, superficially more interesting, illustrates again Mackintosh taking refuge in tradition, as represented by the rural ladderback chairs of Ernest Gimson.
(*Victoria and Albert Museum*)

32. This Mackintosh drawing for an easy chair in a dining room illustrates the difficulty progressive designers had in creating upholstered furniture that would be at once original and aesthetically satisfying. (*Glasgow University*)

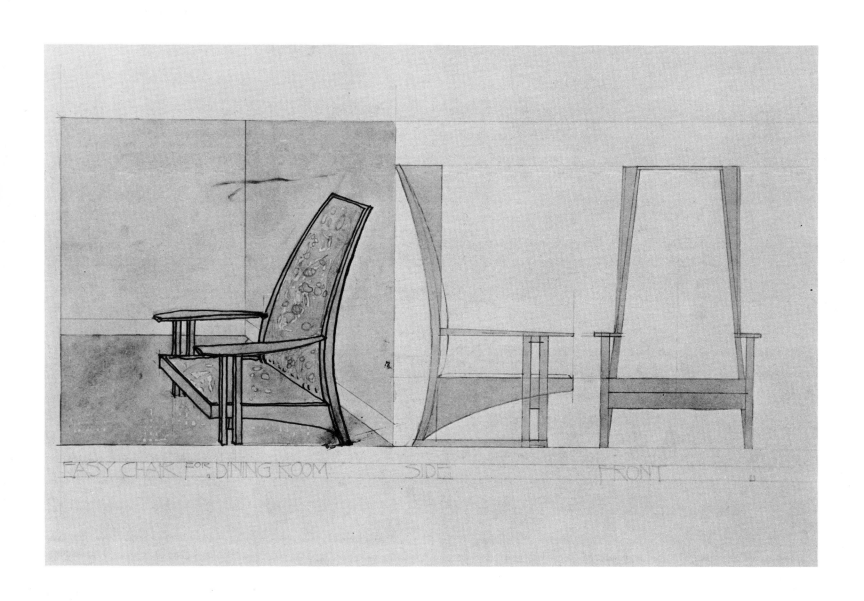

EASY CHAIR FOR DINING ROOM   SIDE   FRONT

33. Apparently after some improvisation, the finished chair, now in Hill House, is more interesting than the design.
(*Photograph   Victor Albrow*)

34. Another unexpected piece of dining room furniture, one of a pair of settles designed by John Ednie for the Wylie and Lochhead pavilion in the Glasgow exhibition of 1901. Although the influence of E. A. Taylor is evident the deeply carved rose and the convex carving below it are typical of Ednie's sculptural orientation.
(Collection William McLean.
Photograph   Victor Albrow)

35. This photograph, taken from a Wylie and Lochhead catalogue, shows more furniture in Ednie's exhibition dining room. The chair on the left is clearly en suite with the settle, but the sideboard, elaborately carved with figures of the four seasons as well as with floral motifs, is scarcely characteristic of Ednie. The interest is in the fussy detail of the piece rather than its shape, perhaps because the designer was inhibited by having to provide furniture compatible with Burne-Jones' splendid but, as far as the Glasgow school was concerned, outmoded tapestry. Superior later designs will be found when we reach the bedroom.
(*Glasgow University*)

36, 37. Two presumably slightly later interior designs by Ednie (not Jane Fonie—see introduction) shown in the Scottish section of the Turin International Exhibition in 1902. They are more characteristic of the designer and his work for the Glasgow Exhibition: the Mackintosh influence is stronger, the Baillie Scott influence is evident in the inglenook frieze of the dining room, and the Ednie personality is visible too in the chair at the table in the same room, in the convex moulding on the cash desk, and in the twin-turreted fireplace in the tearoom. The tearoom chairs are to be compared with Ednie's bedroom chair in illustration 22.
(*Sotheby's*)

38. Wylie and Lochhead chairs have a generic identity, possibly because of standards set by E. A. Taylor who designed these inlaid oak dining chairs. Had the designer's name not been known in this case it would not have been possible to attribute them to him with any certainty.
(*University of Glasgow*)

39. A sideboard by E. A. Taylor for the dining room of Lord Weir's house. The pierced patterns in the metal fittings, the shallow carved panels, and the centrally peaked cornice are modifications of early Mackintosh features that became characteristic of Taylor. (*University of Glasgow*)

40. It has been difficult to find Glasgow style dining tables, apart from the beautiful but familiar ones by Mackintosh. Although this table might not have been originally intended for a dining room we illustrate it here as a splendid example of Herbert MacNair's architectural genius. It stands at present in the library at Hill House, where its rough-hewn individuality contrasts with the elegance of the Mackintosh furnishings. It would have been made in the mid-1890s.

(*Photograph   Victor Albrow*)

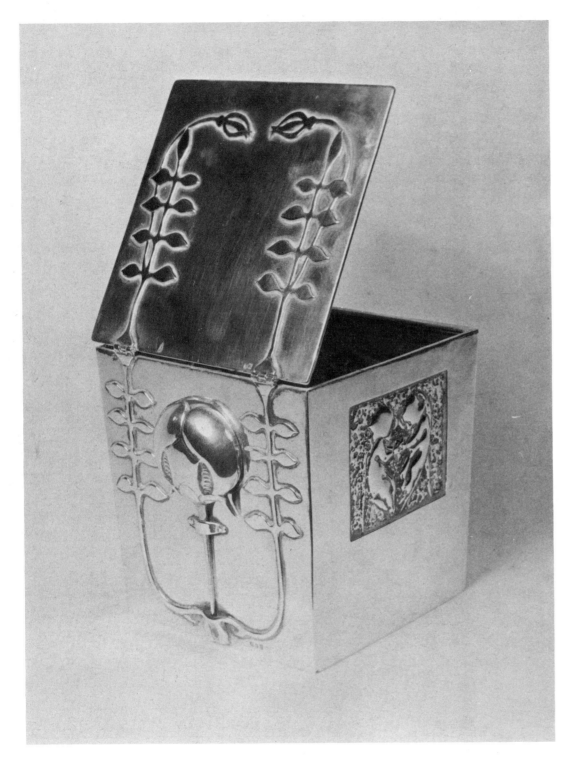

41. A silver tea caddy designed by Herbert MacNair in 1897 for the marriage of his sister. The three-dimensional rose on the side of the box detaches itself to become the caddy spoon. The box is hallmarked, but it is not known precisely who the maker was. It is possible that Frances Macdonald designed and made the side panels.
(Collection Mrs Armstrong.
Photograph   Stephen Daniels)

42. A small plaster panel by Herbert MacNair, the central figure apparently modelled on Frances, showing a very similar arrangement of curves to those of the caddy spoon (opposite), set against a rectangular grid.
(Collection Mrs Armstrong.
Photograph   Stephen Daniels)

43. A silver caddy spoon with the same maker's mark as the tea caddy, presumably designed by either Herbert MacNair or Frances Macdonald. (*Private collection.   Photograph   Victor Albrow*)

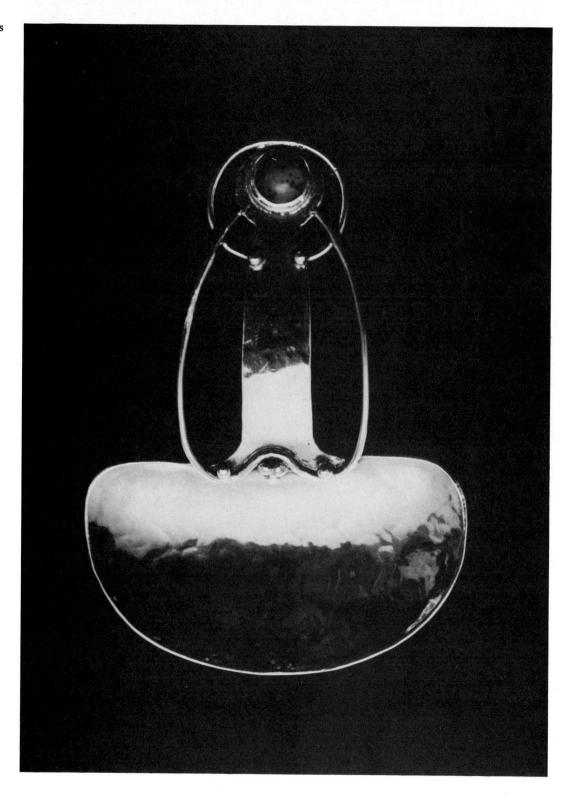

44. Margaret Macdonald Mackintosh's watercolour 'Fantasy' is included at this point to demonstrate how the elliptical curves-within-curves of the Glasgow style can be found in objects as widely differing as a painting and a caddy spoon. Seen in this context the handle of the spoon (overleaf) assumes a stylised human shape. The water colour was bought at the Mackintosh memorial exhibition in 1933 by Jessie King, whose style had been formed by the influence of similar imagery.
(*Sotheby's*)

45. Sugar tongs designed by Herbert MacNair for Miss Mary 'Bee' Phillips as a wedding present in 1906.
(*Walker Art Gallery, Liverpool*)

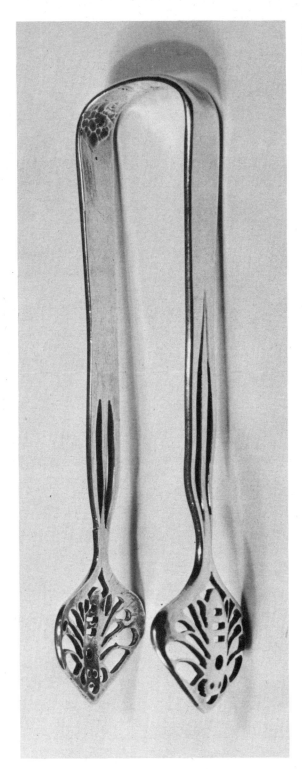

46. Silver spoons and forks designed by Mackintosh for the Newberys circa 1906. Mackintosh elongation is here carried into cutlery design (the soup spoon is 10½ inches long) to make a radical departure from conventional silverware. The pierced motif is art nouveau decoration reduced to its ultimate simplicity.
(Collection Mrs Sturrock.
Photograph Victor Albrow)

48. German fruit knife and fork with bronze handles decorated with geometric patterns and Glasgow roses. The maker is unknown. The Mackintosh rose flowered in several centres in Germany and Austria, but most abundantly in the Darmstadt artist colony where Hans Christiansen for example was known as Rosen-Christiansen for his obsession with them.
(Private collection.   Photograph   Victor Albrow)

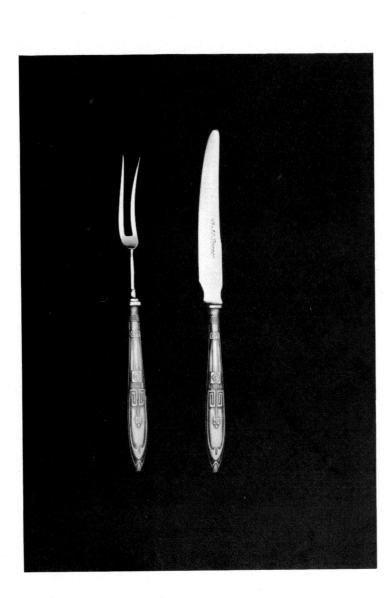

49. A cabinet showing another German adaptation of the Glasgow rose, both in the inlay and in the fine bronze drawer handles. It is similar to several examples of furniture designed by Hans Christiansen.
(*Private collection.   Photograph   Victor Albrow*)

50. Silver cup and cover with enamel medallions by Miss de Courcy Lewthwaite Dewar. Like the clock in the following illustration this piece is more in the English arts and crafts tradition than the Scottish, but Miss Dewar's metalwork was at times strongly influenced by that of Margaret and Frances Macdonald. See the casket and mirror frame in the bedroom section.
(*Collection David Lloyd-Jones.*
Photograph Victor Albrow)

51. Metal clock with enamel face and decorative panel attributed to Miss de Courcy Lewthwaite Dewar.
(*Collection William McLean.*
Photograph Victor Albrow)

52. This tiny liqueur glass designed by Herbert MacNair and possibly made in Clutha glass by James Couper of Glasgow seems not to be complete. Once the rose bowl was complemented by tendril leaves rising from the foot. It was exhibited at the Education Exhibition in St George's Hall, Liverpool, 1901, as part of a suite including also finger bowls and spirit tumblers.
(*Collection Mrs Armstrong.*
Photograph ***Stephen Daniels***)

53. A useful contemporary photograph of the George Walton section in an exhibition, showing examples of his Clutha glass, together with his Venetian style glass for James Powell, and the three-branched 'Cawdor' candlesticks, on a walnut sideboard. The outcurved legs of the sideboard are very characteristic of the designer.

54. One of several Clutha glass vases designed for James Couper by George Walton. He also designed glassware for James Powell of Whitefriars in a frilly pastiche of the Venetian manner which has nothing to do with the Glasgow style.
(*Private collection.   Photograph   Victor Albrow*)

55. Part of a tea-set designed by George Logan for the Staffordshire firm Foley Art China, Peacock pottery, circa 1903. The motif on this set appears as a wall decoration in the Logan bedroom illustrated at number 143. Wylie and Lochhead retailed a wide range of household goods and it is possible that they commissioned Staffordshire firms to make up the designs of their artists.
(*Private collection.   Photograph   Victor Albrow*)

56, 57. More examples of Foley china with transfer decoration attributed to George Logan. The 'Swastika Ware' milk jug was, of course, designed when the swastika was still an innocent Celtic symbol. The chequer border on the cup and saucer may be compared with that on the ewer and basin in the bedroom section.
(Collection David Lloyd Jones.
Photograph Victor Albrow)
(Private collection. Photograph Stephen Daniels)

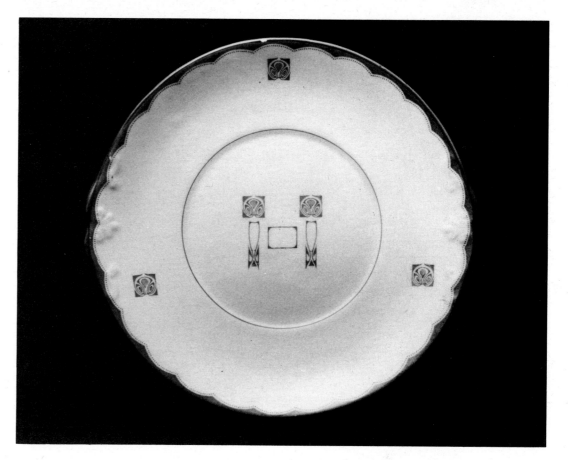

58. A Glasgow style decoration incongruously imposed on a conventionally shaped Staffordshire earthenware tureen in blue and white, and bearing the title 'Tulip Ware'.
(*Private collection.   Photograph   Victor Albrow*)

59. The hand-painted pottery of Jessie King is in a quite different tradition from the mass-produced Staffordshire china. Each one of her pieces carries its own design in spite of the fact that she went on producing them for years as tourist ware in Kirkcudbright.
(*Private collection. Photograph Victor Albrow*)

60. It seems, on the evidence of the monogram on this vase, that E. A. Taylor occasionally contributed to the stock of painted pottery on sale in Kirkcudbright. This particular one has stencilled decoration, and is dated 1925. (*Private collection. Photograph Victor Albrow*)

61. Part of a tea-set hand painted by Miss de Courcy Lewthwaite Dewar. Unlike Jessie King's pottery the shapes appear to have been designed by the artist. Jessie King usually painted on factory-made blanks. (*Collection David Lloyd Jones. Photograph Victor Albrow*)

62. E. A. Taylor's doorplate for the drawing-room of Lord Weir's house. (*Contemporary photograph*)

63. Two views of the drawing room designed by E. A. Taylor for the Wylie and Lochhead pavilion in the Glasgow exhibition of 1901. An excellent example of Taylor's marriage of the Edwardian and Glasgow styles. It is instructive to compare the white screens which divide the room with the side of the John Ednie settle, illustration 34. Ednie seems to have taken the inlaid hearts from Taylor's repertoire as well as the grouped verticals and general shape of the screen for his settle, but there is a pronounced individuality in the carved rose in Ednie's top panel and in the more imaginative moulding below it.

(*Contemporary photograph*)

64. Another view of the room illustrated overleaf.
(*Contemporary photograph*)

65. Perhaps the most attractive of the Taylor furniture shown at the Glasgow exhibition was this hexagonal occasional table, its sides sensitively inlaid with pansies and heart-shaped leaves, the curved apron pierced with split hearts. This piece owes little to Mackintosh, much to Baillie Scott and to commercial English art nouveau.
(Collection William McLean.
Photograph   Victor Albrow)

66. Part of a room in the Scottish section of the
Turin International Exhibition, 1902, showing
a cabinet and a small table by E. A. Taylor,
and a metal mirror frame by Talwyn Morris.
It is interesting that only a year after the
Glasgow Exhibition Taylor's furniture, though
still recognisably his, is so much more
distinctively Glasgow in style. This was
perhaps the first time that Taylor and
Mackintosh exhibited together, and the latter's
influence is particularly evident in the stained
glass panels. The same metal fittings are to be
found on other art nouveau furniture
manufactured by Wylie and Lochhead. It
would be interesting to know who designed
the flower vase: Mackintosh is known to have
designed pottery, but we have not yet found
any examples of it.
(*Contemporary photograph*)

67. Another of E. A. Taylor's Turin exhibits, this screen with the non-geometric complex of curves in the stained glass panels is even more stylish.
(*Contemporary photograph*)

69. A screen by George Logan, as exhibited at the Turin Exhibition in 1902.
(*Contemporary photograph*)

68. Although this dark-stained cabinet was sold with the contents of E. A. Taylor's studio in 1977, and attributed to him, it is questionable whether he ever achieved this degree of sophistication. This is clearly not a Wylie and Lochhead product, and the way in which the doors are extended downwards to form a pendant motif has something in common with an early Mackintosh design.
(*Sotheby's*)

70. A detail of the screen in 69. Considering that it has been to Australia and back, and that it has escaped a serious fire, it is still in very good condition, as this detail shows. The silver rods across the vesica opening, and the chains with pearls and turquoises from above it, are missing, but the silver hearts and roses, and the pearls and other stones, are perfectly preserved. The screen was executed by Wylie and Lochhead, and it incorporates several generic features which are nevertheless typical of George Logan's work rather than Taylor's.
(Collection Patrick Higson. Photograph Victor Albrow)

71. The screen is a very apt setting for Jessie King's water-colour 'Princesses of the Red Rose' which occupies the central panel. (*Collection Patrick Higson.* *Photograph Victor Albrow*)

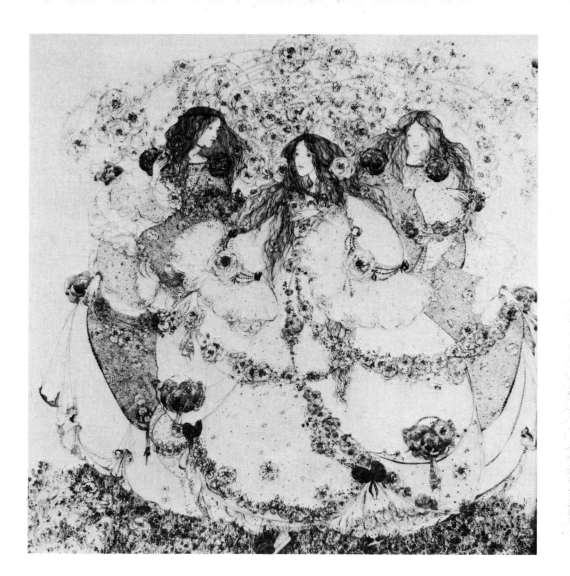

72. A drawing for a fireplace by Jessie King, one of her few interior designs. (*Sotheby's*)

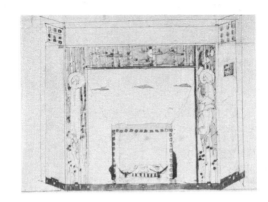

73. Formerly attributed to Jessie King, this interior design is clearly not by the same hand as the fireplace above. Although it has a feminine appearance it lacks Jessie King's fantasy, and is almost certainly by George Logan, who published several similar designs in *The Studio*. It is Mackintosh elaborated into a suburban ideal of prettiness. The butterflies on the frieze are not exclusive to Logan, but they appear in many designs known to be by him. (*Sotheby's*)

74, 75. Two fabric designs, 'Kingcup' and 'Rose', by Jessie King, made either for Liberty's or Wylie and Lochhead. (*Sotheby's*)

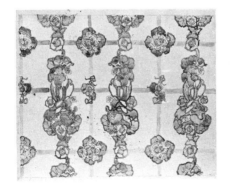

76. Design by Mackintosh for a standard lamp, the shades incorporating in stained glass the split-heart motif which he originated, and which E. A. Taylor wholeheartedly adopted. (*Glasgow University*)

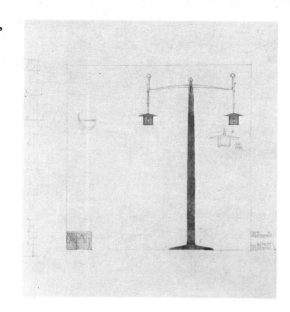

77. Mackintosh's design for a lampshade in Hill House.

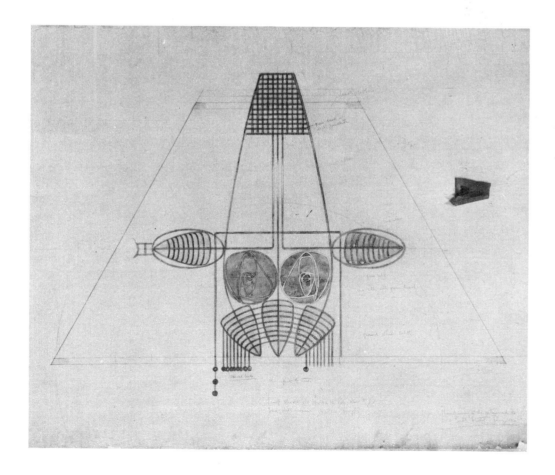

78. The finished shade as executed by Margaret Macdonald Mackintosh in the twenties to replace the outworn original (now partially preserved in the Victoria and Albert Museum). (*Photograph Victor Albrow*)

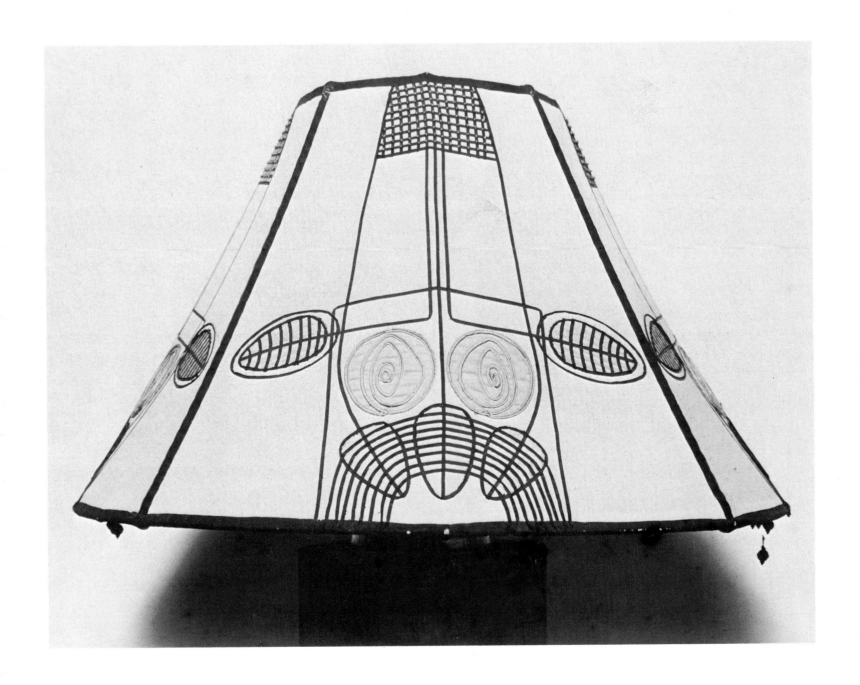

79. E. A. Taylor's Ladies' Room in The King's Head Hotel, Sheffield, 1902, showing an interesting light fitting, and elegant furniture designed for the English taste, but with Scottish stained glass in the door, and the Taylor signature of split hearts in the desk on the right. (*Contemporary photograph*)

80. Another room by Taylor, possibly in the same hotel, with an extravagantly Scottish light fitting and some fairly clumsy upholstered furniture. (*Contemporary photograph*)

81. Mackintosh also had difficulty with upholstered furniture. This sofa was designed for the smoking room in the Argyle Street tearooms.
(*University of Glasgow*)

82. Progressive designers of the period were more successful with sofas with bare wooden frames, as in this example by E. A. Taylor in his drawing room for the Coats' house in Birmingham, 1901. The frieze in this room is a pattern which can be found on Wylie and Lochhead chairs attributed variously to Taylor and George Logan.
(*Glasgow Museum and Art Gallery*)

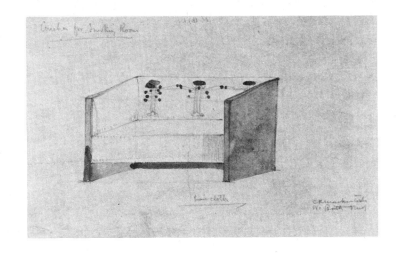

83. A very much more self-conscious drawing room, designed by George Walton on his best behaviour for A. S. Ball's exhibition of interiors in 1907. Although German critics of the time found the seating inhospitably low, they preferred this room to Mackintosh's stark dining room.
(*Contemporary photograph*)

84. George Walton was responsible for one of the most beautiful of Liberty's drawing room chairs.
(*Victoria and Albert Museum*)

85. Walton also designed for J. S. Henry, the leading art furnishers in London. This cabinet is illustrated in *The Studio Yearbook* for 1908, where it is said to be designed and executed by J. S. Henry, who at this late date were no longer acknowledging their individual designers. There are several Glasgow features in this cabinet—the squares of copper and opaque glass, the style of the leading, and the enamel disc. These, combined with specific Walton characteristics such as the curved upper windows, the egg-shaped central panel with square-notched border, the prominent cornice, and above all the elongated hinges with their white glass inserts, make it seem possible that George Walton designed the piece.
(*Private collection.   Photograph   Victor Albrow*)

86. An impressive cabinet by George Walton in his upper-middle style, made for The Philippines, Brasted, Kent in 1902. Its Scottish origin is visible only in the gilded squares under the cornice.
(*Collection Angus Grossart.*
Photograph Victor Albrow)

87. It is possible that Walton also designed for Goodyer's of Regent Street—see caption to illustration no. 28. This clock was sold by them, and again the Scottish features such as the long-stemmed enamelled rectangles suggest a Walton influence.
(Private collection. Photograph Victor Albrow)

88. There are Walton characteristics too in this Scottish coal-holder in polished steel with stained glass panels. It could, however, equally well have been made by the Scottish Guild of Handicrafts, some of whose table lamps, as illustrated in *The Studio*, are equally stylish. (*Private collection.   Photograph   Victor Albrow*)

89. Two fireplace designs by John Ednie, submitted under the pseudonym 'Severity' to *Studio* competitions in 1901 and 1903. Both fireplaces show the influence of Baillie Scott, in the long-stemmed plants with twin leaves in the 1901 design, and in the plump birds in flight in the 1903 design. Unlike his Wylie and Lochhead colleagues Ednie frequently used squares in his designs, as in the surround of the later fireplace. Both designs received only an honourable mention.

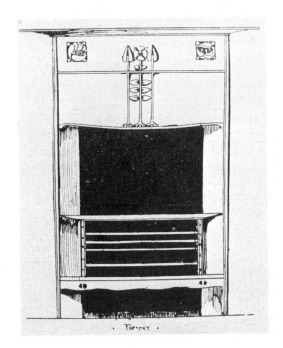

91, 92, 93. Three fireplaces designed by E. A. Taylor for Lord Weir's house. The first shows, as well as a Liberty clock, two stained glass cupboard doors typical of his imaginative use of this medium.
(*University of Glasgow, 91*)
(*Contemporary photograph, 92*)
(*Contemporary photograph, 93*)

94. A Jessie King bookcover of 1905 which has everything—the roses, the butterflies, the birds in flight, the little squares—all derived from Mackintosh, but combined here with one of the artist's fairy figures. In common with most Glasgow covers it has nothing to do with the contents of the book, but represents a virtuoso self-indulgence on the part of the artist in her favourite motifs. It relates closely to the jewellery she designed for Liberty's. (*Private collection. Photograph Stephen Daniels*)

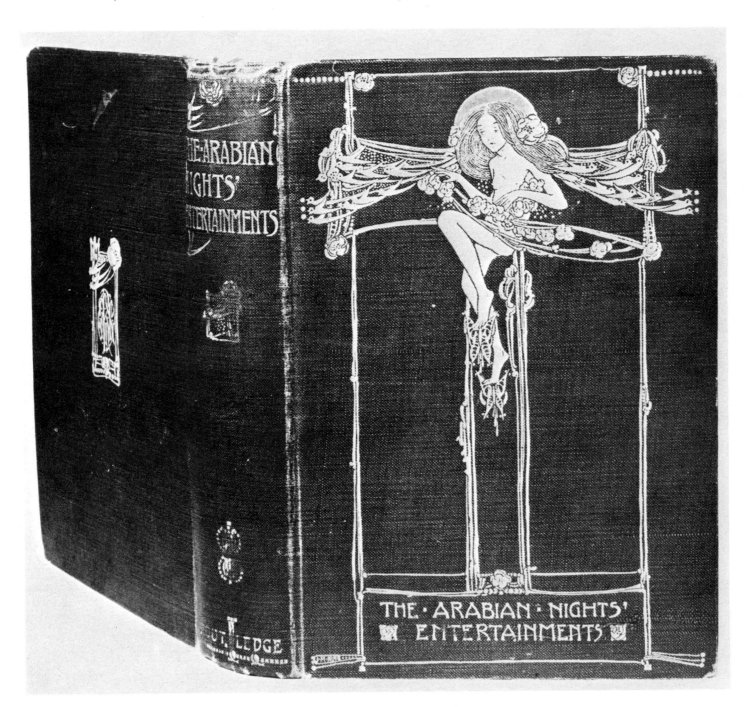

95. Dating from five years before the bookcover opposite, this bookplate shows Jessie King as close as she ever came to the source of her inspiration. Although the figures are already more charming and less disturbing than those in the early drawings of Margaret and Frances Macdonald the overall design possesses the authentic Glasgow style vitality. (*Sotheby's*)

96. A vivid example of how widespread Jessie King's reputation had become by 1900, this cover for an album of photographs of Berlin is a startling combination of Glasgow hearts and flowers with symbols of German imperialism. It no doubt looked less incongruous to the readers of the time than it does to us today. (*Private collection*)

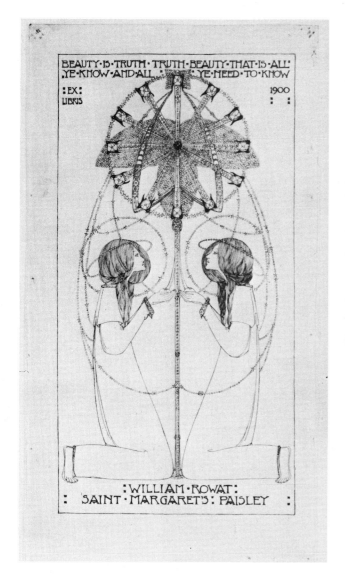

97. Two examples of bookplates by Miss de Courcy Lewthwaite Dewar.
(*Contemporary photograph*)

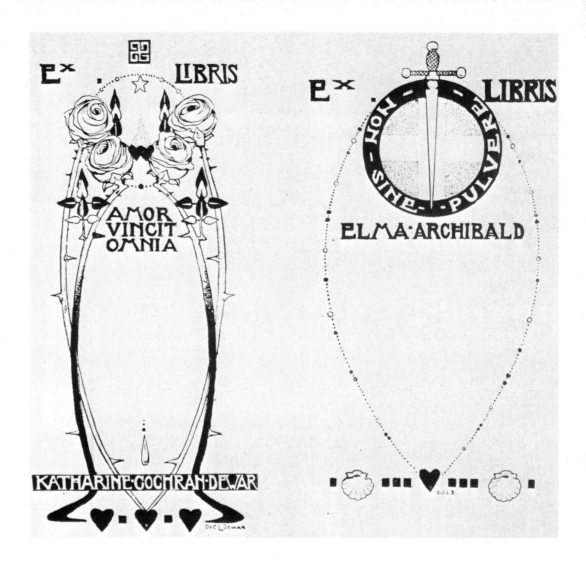

98. A bookcase designed by Talwin Morris for his house at Bowling, illustrated in *The Studio* in 1900. The construction is unremarkable, but the metal fittings are attractively designed and finely executed.
(*Contemporary photograph*)

99. Three mirror frames by Talwin Morris, all excellent examples of his imaginative metalwork. The flattened hearts in the mirror on the right are a characteristic Talwin Morris adaptation of a familiar motif. The eye in the frame on the left, derived from the Macdonald sisters' wall sconce, here has a wittily surreal effect.
(*Contemporary photograph*)

100. The metal panel of this wall sconce in Hill House was designed and made by Talwin Morris for his employer Walter Blackie, who commissioned the house from Mackintosh following Morris's recommendation. (*Photograph   Victor Albrow*)

101. The attribution of this repoussé metal panel to Talwin Morris is open to doubt. However the face could only be by someone familiar with the early work of the Four, and the linear pattern surrounding it has much in common with other Morris designs. *(Collection John Jesse. Photograph   Stephen Daniels)*

102. A Talwin Morris bookcover for Blackie and Son with a simple linear pattern similar to that in the preceding illustration.
(*Private collection.   Photograph   Victor Albrow*)

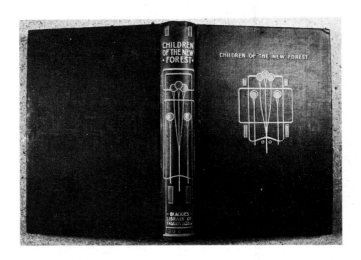

103. One of Talwin Morris's many bookcovers for Blackie and Son, one a disciplined vignette.
(*Private collection.*
Photograph   Victor Albrow)

104. Another Talwin Morris bookcover for Blackie and Son, a riot of Glasgow and other art nouveau motifs.
(*Private collection.   Photograph   Victor Albrow*)

105. The Secessionist austerity of this 1911 drawing for a gravestone for Talwin Morris by Mackintosh contrasts sadly with the vitality of the natural forms of the Glasgow style. (*Glasgow University*)

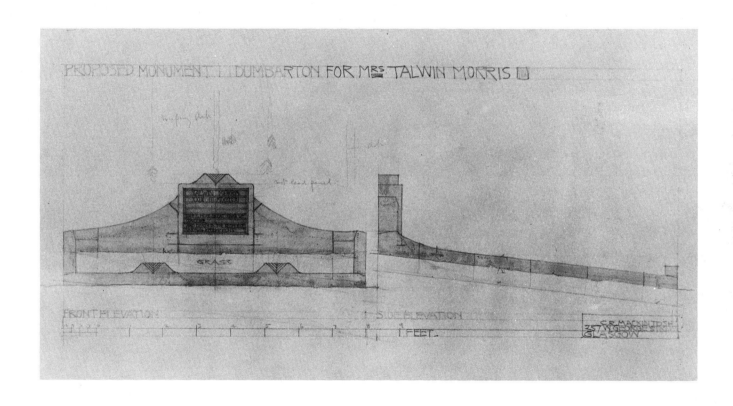

106. Tapestry design by Otto Prutscher illustrated in *The Studio Yearbook* 1907. (*Contemporary illustration*)

107. It has been shown that Mackintosh borrowed ideas from Otto Prutscher—which was no more than taking back what he had given Vienna years before—for his interiors at 78 Derngate. The close similarity between the Prutscher tapestry below and this Blackie's bookcover of the early 1920s seems to confirm that Mackintosh did in fact produce the designs commissioned from him by Walter Blackie at this time. An unfinished sketch for a Henty cover, with a design based on squares, is preserved in the Glasgow University Mackintosh Collection.
(*Private collection.   Photograph   Victor Albrow*)

108. The Rossetti Library designed by George Logan for the Wylie and Lochhead pavilion in the Glasgow Exhibition 1901. The bookcase from this library survives; it was once in the Handley-Read Collection and is now in the Victoria and Albert Museum.
(*Contemporary photograph*)

109. A corner of the writing room designed by Herbert and Frances MacNair for the Turin Exhibition in 1902. Both the chair and the revolving bookcase inspired similar furniture by Mackintosh. The flower arrangements of the Four were famous, often twisted out of long brambles and twigs, with the addition of paper blooms. No garden flowers would be so amenable to the Glasgow style.
(*Contemporary photograph*)

110. A very early Glasgow style cabinet by Herbert MacNair, signed and dated 1895, and made for his own office in Glasgow. It is a large and heavy piece of furniture, enlivened by its hand-made metal fittings, particularly the pierced face which backs the handle on the side door. The fittings were originally polished rather than painted black as they are now. (*Walker Art Gallery, Liverpool. Photograph Stephen Daniels*)

111. Detail of MacNair cabinet.

112. An attractive mahogany desk designed by E. A. Taylor for Wylie and Lochhead, who illustrated it in their catalogue, circa 1903. (*Collection William McLean. Photograph Victor Albrow*)

113. A strange little desk identifiable as Wylie and Lochhead by the carving between the drawers and the handles, and tentatively attributable to George Logan.
(*Collection David Lloyd Jones.*
Photograph   Victor Albrow)

114. A design for one of the centre lamps in the smoking room of the Argyle Street tearooms. Mackintosh never used a decorative motif lightly, and his notes here indicate that the drops of purple glass, representing the fruit of the olive tree—'the flower of peace'—had a symbolic meaning for him.
(*University of Glasgow*)

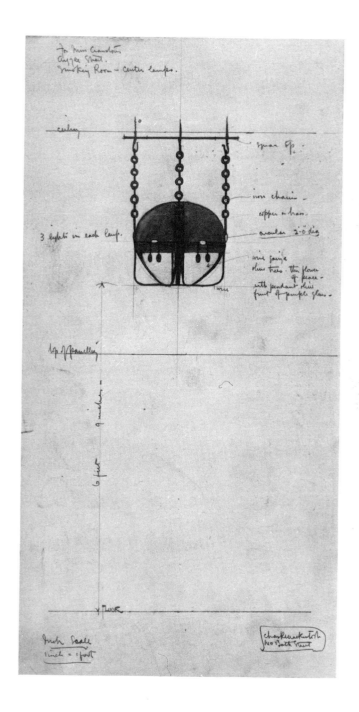

115. A magazine rack formerly attributed to Mackintosh because of its similarity to one in the School of Art, Glasgow, but now in doubt because of the unsatisfactory provenance of the latter. Numerous variations of this design exist, some closer and some further away from a presumed Glasgow original.
(*Private collection.   Photograph   Victor Albrow*)

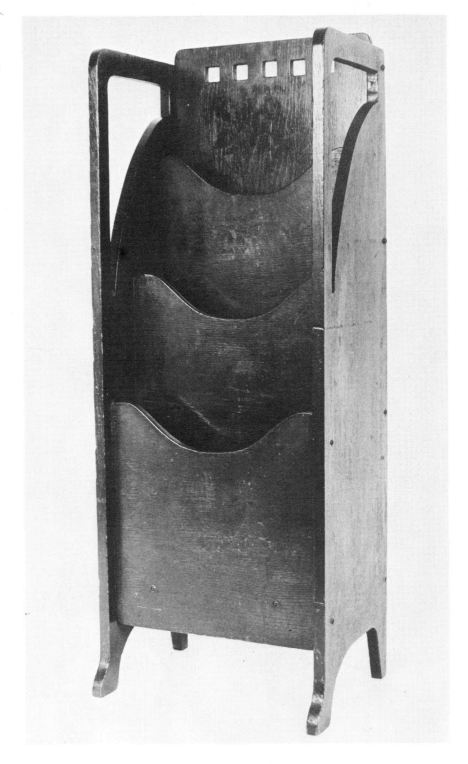

116. A late example of Glasgow influence in an oak library table with relief decoration of chequers and verticals on the central supports. (*Private collection. Photograph Victor Albrow*)

117. A domino table designed by Mackintosh for Miss Cranston's Argyle Street tearooms in 1897. There are several variants of this table, some of them not by Mackintosh. (*Victoria and Albert Museum*)

118. One of a set of chairs designed for the card-room in Miss Cranston's home at Hous'hill, this is a fascinating example of Mackintosh's interest at this time in traditional English furniture. His sketchbook shows a carefully measured study of a Windsor chair at Chiddingstone, some of the features of which—notably the arrangement of the spindles in the back, and the swollen joints of the stretchers—are incorporated in the card-room chair, together with such distinctively personal features as the squared relief decoration on the legs, and the curved top rail.
(Private collection. Photograph Victor Albrow)

119. Mackintosh's first high-backed chair, designed for the Argyle Street tearooms in 1897, has a distinct priestly authority. Mackintosh was preoccupied with symbolism, and it is not unlikely that some such picture as 'The Druids' inspired this radical departure from traditional chair design. (*Contemporary photograph*)

120. 'The Druids: Bringing in the Mistletoe', painted by E. A. Hornel and George Henry in 1890, is an important source of Glasgow style symbolism. It was influential, not so much because of its Celtic detail, as because of its ritual atmosphere, the hieratic arrangement of the figures, and the totemic imagery.
(*Glasgow Museum and Art Gallery*)

121. Mackintosh's poster for *The Musical Review* (1896) combines a druidic figure with Celtic symbols similar to those in the Hornel/Henry painting, together with his characteristic branching uprights and symbolic singing birds.
(*University of Glasgow*)

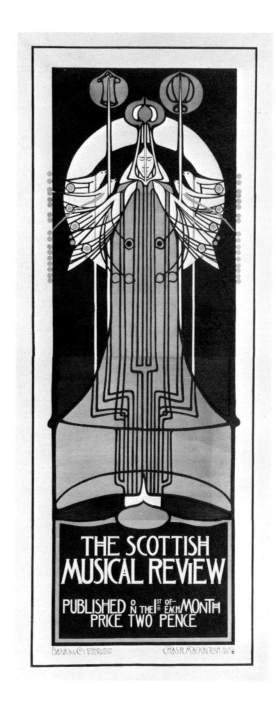

122. An earlier (circa 1886) high-backed chair by the English architect A. H. Mackmurdo of the Century Guild. This interesting chair certainly has a ceremonial character, but it has nothing of the poetic excitement of Mackintosh's chair. (*Private collection.   Photograph   Victor Albrow*)

123. Perhaps the earliest 'art' chair was designed by Holman Hunt in 1855 for his own use, after an ancient Egyptian original, which was later also the source of one of the Liberty Thebes stools. This version of the Holman Hunt chair, executed by Gillows, lacks his elaborate inlay, and is probably one of the pair that Ford Madox Brown had copied, with the permission of his fellow artist. The interest of the Preraphaelite artists and their associates in chair design was no doubt encouraged by William Morris. Rosetti designed one of Morris's most successful chairs in 1866, and in a Burne-Jones tapestry designed for Morris, and illustrated in *The Studio* in 1894, there are two interesting ideas for chairs, one of which was taken up by Baillie Scott.
(*Private collection.   Photograph   Victor Albrow*)

124. Baillie Scott was quite candid about the derivation of this chair, which was made for the Duke of Hesse-Darmstadt in 1897 from Burne-Jones' tapestry.
(*Victoria and Albert Museum*)

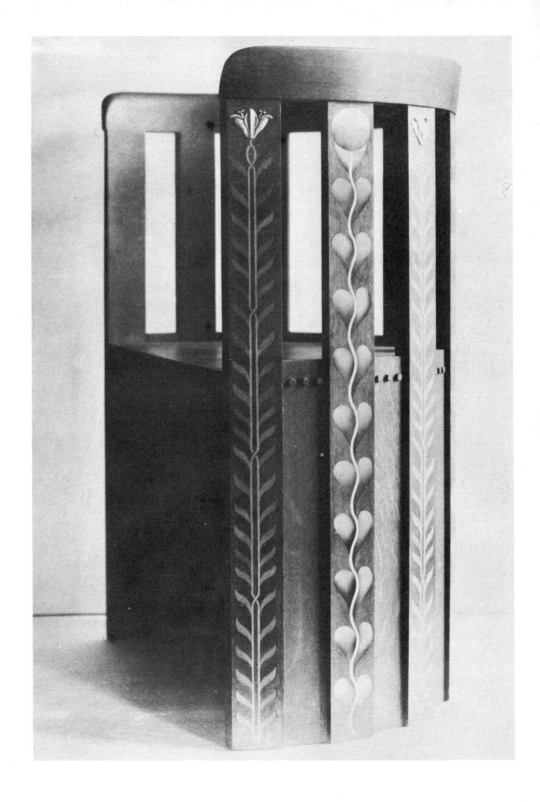

125. A Mackintosh totem, one of several towering above the railing outside the School of Art, Glasgow.
(*Photograph   Victor Albrow*)

126. Agnes Raeburn was a member of the Mackintosh circle at the School of Art, and her poster for the Glasgow Lecture Association (1897 or before) is one of the few designs from that group making use of basic Celtic motifs such as the snake and the entrelac. (*University of Glasgow*)

127. Another, later, example of a Celtic design by a pupil of the Glasgow School of Art, Mary R. Henderson.
(*Private collection.   Photograph   Victor Albrow*)

128. A preoccupation with Celtic motifs was more common with the East coast Scottish artists, such as James Cromer Watt, the Aberdeen jeweller and enamellist, who made this exquisite silver box with enamel decoration cloisonné in gold, inset with cabochon gemstones.
(*Private collection.   Photograph   Victor Albrow*)

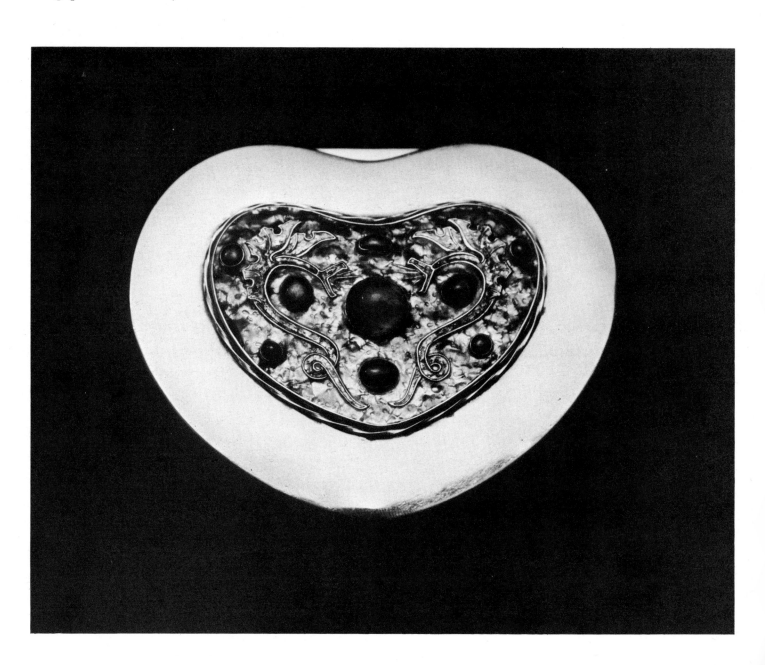

129. Aubrey Beardsley was a major source of inspiration for the Glasgow artists, as is demonstrated by this wooden box stylishly painted in gesso by Mary Newbery (now Mrs Sturrock), daughter of the headmaster of the School of Art.
(*Collection Mrs Sturrock.*
Photograph   Victor Albrow)

130. David Gauld's painting 'Saint Agnes', 1889, with its lonely, elongated figure in a tapestry landscape, is a remarkably early anticipation of the Glasgow style. (*Collection A. McIntosh Patrick*)

131. Frances Macdonald's 'Ill Omen', dated 1893, created a new atmosphere and a new symbolism with scarcely any precedents or external influences.
(*University of Glasgow*)

132. 'The Lovers', a watercolour by Herbert MacNair, was painted about the same time as 'Ill-Omen' and is clearly related to it, in spite of its characteristic proliferating detail. (*Collection Mrs Armstrong.* *Photograph Stephen Daniels*)

133. Portrait of Herbert MacNair by Enid Jackson, who is thought to have been one of his pupils in Liverpool.
(*Walker Art Gallery, Liverpool*)

134. 'The Legend of St Christopher', a Christmas card by Herbert MacNair, printed, gilt-embossed, and hand coloured. A later example of MacNair's proliferating symbolism.
(*Collection Mrs Armstrong.*
Photograph   Stephen Daniels)

135. Annie French's Christmas card—another manifestation of Beardsley's influence on the Glasgow artists—was produced in exactly the same way as MacNair's.
(*Private collection.   Photograph   Stephen Daniels*)

136. Two examples of MacNair's graphic work in Liverpool. In the three years after the poster opposite the image of Frances has lost its mystery, although the flying birds present in MacNair's earliest designs are still there in 1904.
(*Both Walker Art Gallery, Liverpool*)

137. MacNair's design for a Liverpool Academy poster.

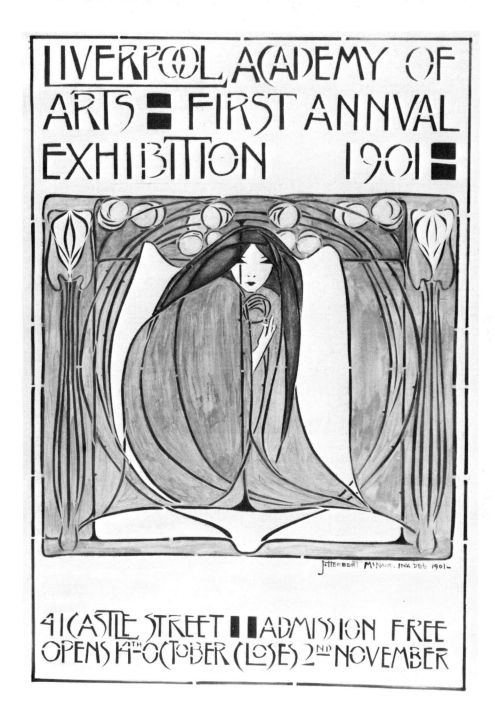

138. This attractive drawing by E. A. Taylor makes an instructive contrast with the MacNair designs we have seen before, and explains why Taylor's lesser talent had so much more commercial success.
(*University of Glasgow*)

139. The puzzling thing about this large Della Robbia vase made at Harold Rathbone's Birkenhead pottery in 1904 is that the very evident Scottish influence in the sgraffito design seems to derive from an earlier (pre-Liverpool) stage in the development of the Glasgow style. It is signed by Cassandia Ann Walker, who was a pupil of MacNair in Liverpool. She was the most talented of the Della Robbia decorators and was often employed to interpret the designs of other artists, which she transferred to stock blanks. It is perhaps not irrelevant to recall at this point that Mackintosh visited Liverpool in 1902, in connection with the Liverpool Cathedral project. Another Glasgow style Della Robbia vase, signed by Cassandia Walker, is dated 1903.
(*Private collection.   Photograph   Victor Albrow*)

140. Mackintosh's 1893 design for a diploma represents the kind of imagery from which the Glasgow style Della Robbia vases seem to derive, although the latter were produced ten years later. The diploma is a vivid example of the way Mackintosh developed his geometric style directly from espalier plant forms.
(*University of Glasgow*)

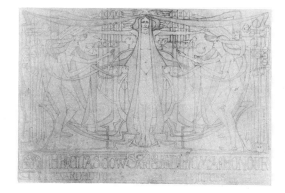

141. An example of the painted ceramic sculpture which flourished in Glasgow in the 1920s. This group is by Jessie Keppie, Mackintosh's first fiancée, who was jilted by him and never married. It is touching to recall that she was present at the Mackintosh Memorial Exhibition in 1933, where she bought a water colour. So, incidentally, did Miss De Courcy Lewthwaite Dewar. (*Private collection.   Photograph   Stephen Daniels*)

142. Embroidered panel by Ann Macbeth 'The
Sleeping Beauty'.
*(Collection William McLean.
Photograph   Victor Albrow)*

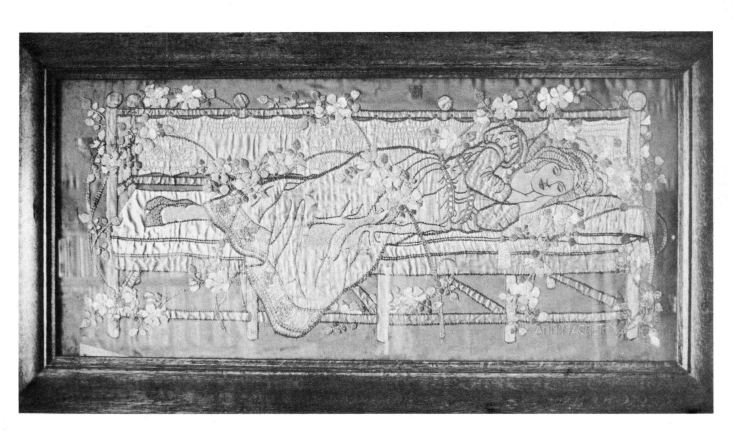

143. A watercolour bedroom in purple and white by George Logan for Wylie and Lochhead, 1903. A characteristically fanciful but not too impractical design, unlike some of his watercolour interiors reproduced in *The Studio*.

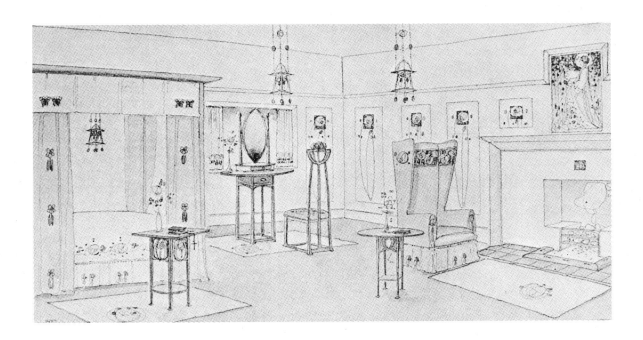

144. It would appear from this basin and ewer in purple, white and yellow, with the same rose motif as in the wall decoration of the above drawing, that the bedroom was indeed put into production. The basin and ewer were made by Wedgwood and Co., presumably to George Logan's design. The same motif is to be found on one of the Foley tea-sets illustrated in the dining room section.
(*Private collection. Photograph Victor Albrow*)

145. A pewter basin and ewer by George Logan, who was responsible for the bedroom in the Wylie and Lochhead pavilion of the Glasgow International Exhibition in 1901. (*Private collection. Photograph Stephen Daniels*)

146. The washstand designed by George Logan to go with the pewter bedroom set at the Glasgow Exhibition. (*Contemporary photograph*)

147. Another bedroom, from a Wylie and Lochhead catalogue, designed by George Logan, similar to his Exhibition piece but less elaborate and obviously intended for production.

148. A Wylie and Lochhead linen press, unusual for them in that it is veneered in walnut. Most Wylie and Lochhead furniture is in solid oak or mahogany. The harebells in the stained glass panels, and the tiny carved butterflies, are similar to the decoration on the wardrobe in Logan's Exhibition suite, and the design of the press is therefore attributed to him.

(Private collection.   Photograph   Victor Albrow)

149. A Mackintosh design for a linen press. (*University of Glasgow*)

150. Mackintosh's superb design for a bedroom, Westdel, Glasgow, 1900. (*University of Glasgow*)

151. This wardrobe, almost certainly designed by John Ednie for Wylie and Lochhead, must have been modelled on Mackintosh's wardrobe in Westdel. The moulding in the shape of outspread wings, and the rectangular panels below, in Mackintosh's design are reflected in the Wylie and Lochhead wardrobe, which however has its own peculiarities. The short bronze hinges, pierced with a bird design over a red leather backing, are by comparison with Mackintosh's long curved hinges alien to the design, and may well have been taken from Wylie and Lochhead's stock; the handles can be found on several other pieces and were probably designed by E. A. Taylor. On the other hand the curved convex moulding at the bottom of Ednie's wardrobe is both characteristic of him and an acceptable reflection of the moulding above, and the Mackintosh style carving at the centre top is not incongruous.

(*Private collection.   Photograph   Victor Albrow*)

152, 153, 154. Two details of the Ednie wardrobe, and a stained glass panel from a wardrobe designed by E. A. Taylor for the Coate's house in Birmingham. The plump flying birds were one of Baillie Scott's favourite motifs, and go back beyond him to Voysey.
(Private collection. Photograph Victor Albrow, 152, 153)
(Contemporary photograph, 154)

155, 156. The washstand and dressing table from the same Ednie bedroom suite, incorporating the blue inverted hearts, the long-stemmed sunflowers, and the tiny squares also to be found on the wardrobe. The chair just visible in the mirror of the dressing table is illustrated in the dining room section.
(*Private collection.   Photograph   Victor Albrow*)

157, 158. The bedside cabinet and towel rail from the same suite, the latter carved with Gothic exuberance.

In one of their catalogues Wylie and Lochhead advertised bedroom suites at prices ranging from £9 10s. to £250. A suite as handsomely designed and as finely executed as this one must have been somewhere near the top of the range. (*Private collection. Photograph Victor Albrow*)

159. A selection of Wylie and Lochhead chairs,
all probably designed by E. A. Taylor,
illustrating some of his characteristic features
and the breadth of his repertoire.
(Private collection.   Photograph   Victor Albrow)

160. The chair from another Wylie and Lochhead bedroom suite, attributed to John Ednie largely on account of the extensive use of chequer inlay.
(Collection William McLean.
Photograph Victor Albrow)

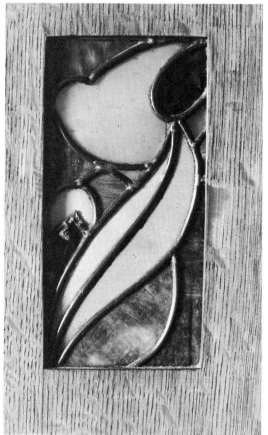

161, 162. The wardrobe in the same suite, with a detail of one of the stained glass panels—another ambiguous bird.
(*Collection William McLean.*
Photograph   Victor Albrow)

163, 164. The very attractive bedhead, and the carved finial at the foot of the bed where Ednie carries his sculptural interest into three dimensions.
(Collection William McLean.
Photograph   Victor Albrow)

165. A fascinating Secessionist design by Mackintosh for a tester bed, dated 1900. Josef Hoffmann in Vienna was doing much the same thing at the same time. (*University of Glasgow*)

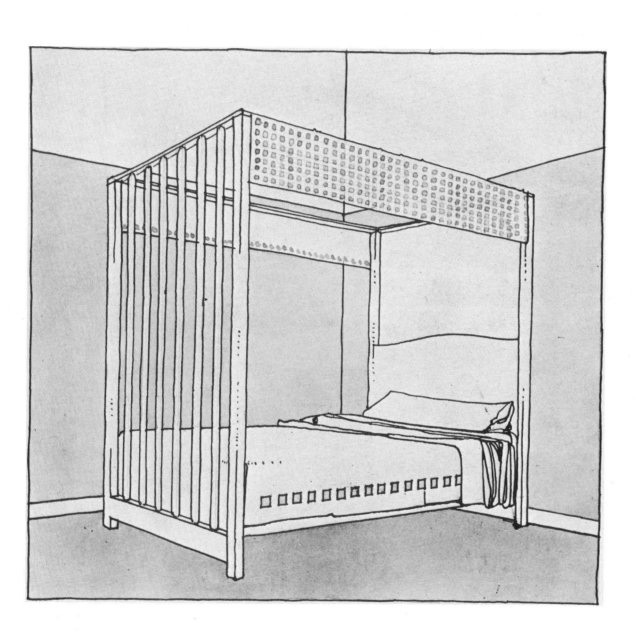

166. Contemporary photograph of one wall of a nursery by Jessie King, who was evidently in her element in fulfilling this commission. It was done for the Musée Galliera Exposition de l'Art pour l'Enfance, circa 1912. (*Sotheby's*)

167. Jessie King's watercolour design for another wall in the same nursery. (*Sotheby's*)

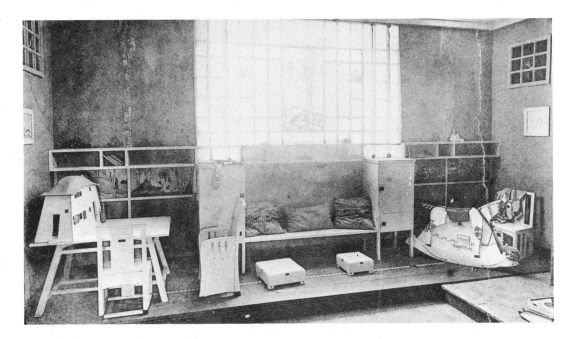

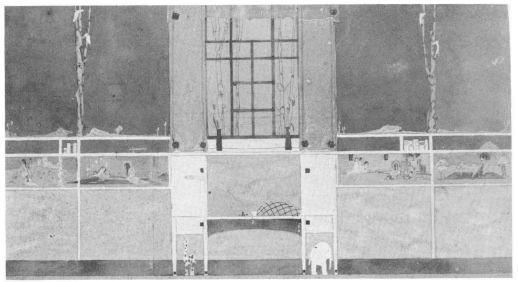

168. A less whimsical design for nursery furniture at Windyhill, Kilmacolm, in 1899 by Mackintosh, who was not incapable of creating sturdy furniture when the occasion demanded it.
(*University of Glasgow*)

169. A view of the Rose Boudoir designed by Mackintosh and Margaret Macdonald Mackintosh for the Scottish section at the Turin Exhibition in 1902.
(*Contemporary photograph*)

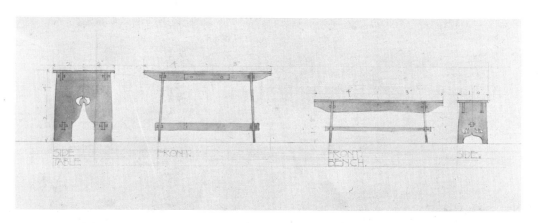

170. A watercolour by Meg Wright dated 1901 of a Glasgow embroideress.
(*Private collection.   Photograph   Victor Albrow*)

171, 172. A cushion cover and a collar and belt designed by Jessie Newbery, wife of the headmaster of the Glasgow School of Art, and one of the leading figures in the Glasgow revival of embroidery as a serious art form. (*Both Victoria and Albert Museum*)

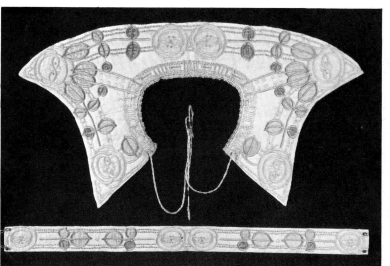

173, 174. A cloth with embroidery designed by
Ann Macbeth, and a cushion cover attributed
to her.
(Victoria and Albert Museum)
(Private collection.   Photograph   Victor Albrow)

175. This bedspread designed by Ann Macbeth, and illustrated in *The Studio Yearbook* in 1911, indicates that this imaginative artist did not restrict herself to the floral motifs of the Glasgow style in its springtime, but that she took her craft forward into abstraction, in line with later progressive trends.

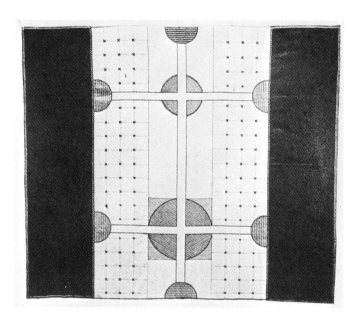

176. An anonymous embroidery, probably by one of the students at the Glasgow School of Art.
(*Collection David Lloyd Jones.*
Photograph   Victor Albrow)

177. An embroidered silk panel almost certainly by Margaret or Frances Macdonald, who were not only a vital inspiration to the Glasgow embroideresses, but who also opened the eyes of Mackintosh and MacNair to the decorative possibilities of this craft. (*Collection David Lloyd Jones. Photograph Victor Albrow*)

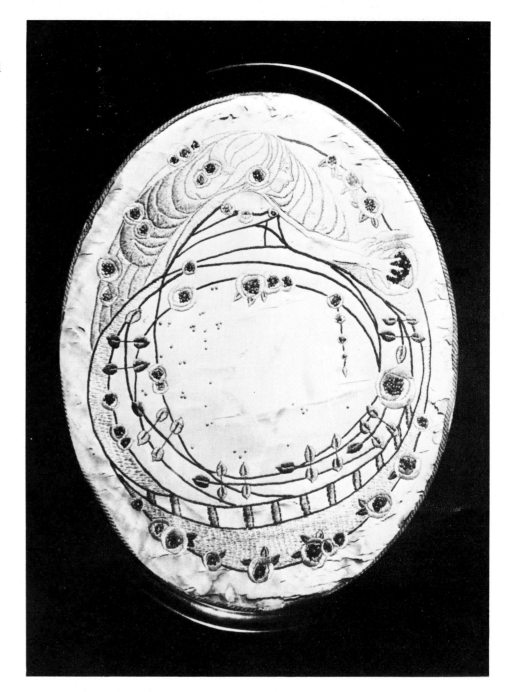

178. Another occupation of artistic Glasgow ladies round the turn of the century was metalwork. Again the inspiration came from Margaret and Frances Macdonald whose extraordinary vision, as exemplified by this 'Honesty' mirror frame (circa 1896) must have been a revelation of what could be achieved in this apparently inflexible medium.
(*Contemporary photograph*)

179. Mackintosh himself also worked in metal for a short time early in his career, when he made this brass casket for his first fiancée, Jessie Keppie.
(*Victoria and Albert Museum*)

180. This picture frame has so much in common with the jewel box by Miss De Courcy Lewthwaite Dewar that it is almost certainly by her. At the same time it owes much to the poetic metalwork of the Macdonald sisters. (*Private collection. Photograph Stephen Daniels*)

181. A jewel box in repoussé metal by Miss De Courcy Lewthwaite Dewar, illustrated in *The Studio* in 1900. (*Collection John Jesse. Photograph Stephen Daniels*)

M

182. Margaret Gilmour, who had studios at West George Street, was a prolific metal worker. She had her own display at the Glasgow Exhibition in 1901, and her early work is done in the Glasgow style, although perhaps over-formalised as in this attractive photograph frame. The faded photograph is of Frances MacNair, wearing a dress apparently of her own design.
(*Collection Stephen Daniels.*
Photograph   Victor Albrow)

183. One of a pair of candlesticks, not signed but attributed to Margaret Gilmour. Similar candlesticks were produced by the Scottish Guild of Handicraft.
(*Private collection.   Photograph   Victor Albrow*)

184, 185. Marion H. Wilson was a particularly talented Glasgow metal worker. The mirror frame with the twin pairs of children's faces is monogrammed by her, and the other, which has much in common with it, can only be attributed to her.
(Both Collection David Lloyd Jones. Photograph   Victor Albrow)

186. A display table for jewellery, one of a pair with sliding side-pieces designed by Herbert MacNair and exhibited at the Turin Exhibition 1902. One contained enamels by Lily Day, none of whose work has come to light as far as we know, and the other displayed what *The Studio* described as 'objets d'art' by the MacNairs. These latter probably included the jewellery illustrated in 'Modern Design in Jewellery and Fans', a *Studio Special Number* published circa 1901, the present whereabouts of which is not known. We believe that Mackintosh and Margaret Macdonald also designed more jewellery than is known at present. Certainly **Mackintosh was known to Josef Hoffmann as a** designer of jewellery, since the Austrian architect invited him to submit jewellery to an exhibition.

Interestingly Mackintosh declined, on the grounds that he could not get pieces made up in time, but recommended his friend Edgar Simpson to him. Some of Simpson's pieces are notably Glasgow, or at least Mackintosh, in style.
*(Collection Mrs Armstrong.
Photograph Stephen Daniels)*

187. A famous piece of jewellery traditionally attributed to Mackintosh and made by Margaret Macdonald. A silver necklace depicting a flight of birds through wirework clouds and seed pearl raindrops.
(Collection Mrs Sturrock)

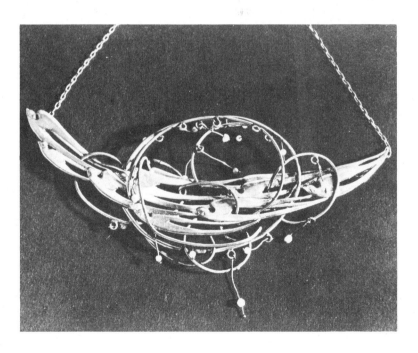

188. This silver gilt brooch is initialled
P.W.D. and, without the wirework clouds,
is illustrated in Peter Wylie Davidson's book
Applied Design in the Precious Metals (1929).
Wylie Davidson taught metalwork and
jewellery at the Glasgow School of Art for
many years. It is believed that this, or a similar
design, was exhibited by him in the Scottish
section at Turin in 1902.
(*Private collection.   Photograph   Victor Albrow*)

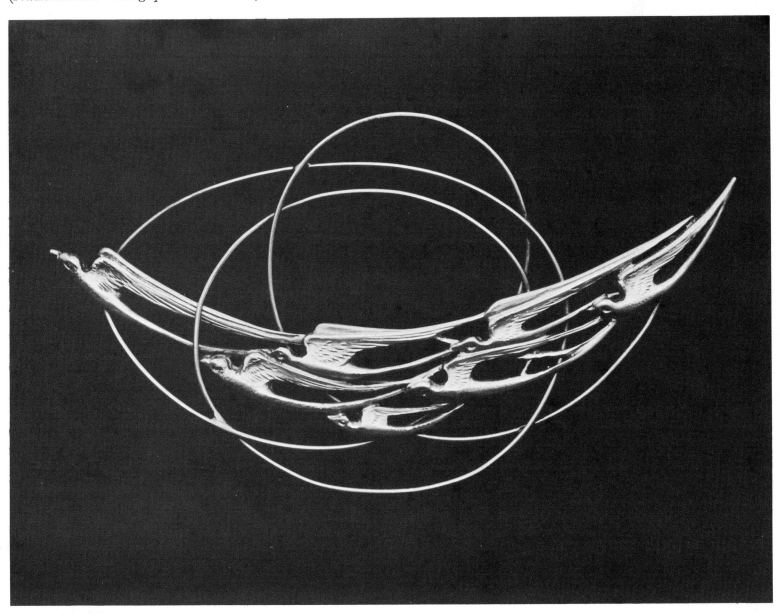

189 (right). This design for a pendant by Kolo Moser, circa 1903, suggests that the Viennese artist knew the jewellery of Mackintosh and Wylie Davidson.

190 (bottom). Two designs by Edgar Simpson, strongly Mackintosh in feeling and technique.

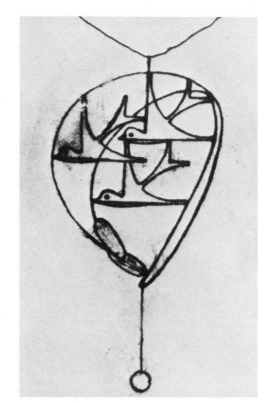

 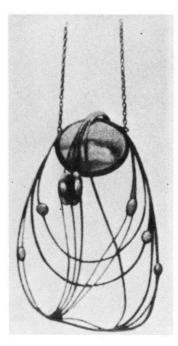

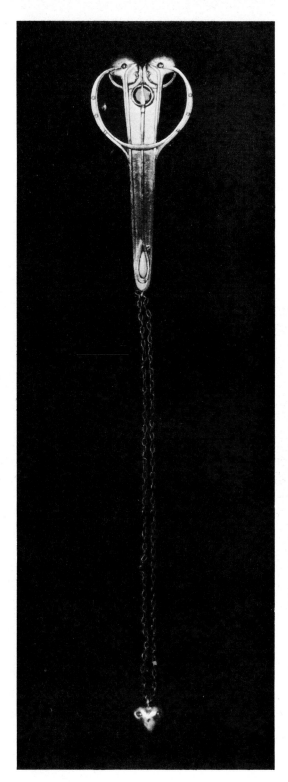

191 A heavy silver brooch with pendant heart set with rubies, pearls and turquoises, designed by Margaret Macdonald for Mrs Newbery after the birth of her second daughter, Mary, in the late 1890s.
(*Collection Mrs Sturrock.*
Photograph   Victor Albrow)

192. A silver and cloisonné enamel brooch with a pattern reminiscent of one of Mackintosh's stained glass vignettes. It could be by Herbert or Frances MacNair, since it bears the same maker's mark as their tea caddy and as the caddy spoon illustrated in the dining room.
(*Private collection.   Photograph   Victor Albrow*)

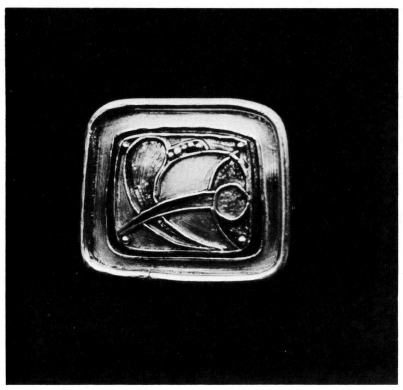

193, 194. Two pieces of silver jewellery by
Mary Thew, a friend of Jessie King and a
resident in the Green Gate Close,
Kirkcudbright.
(*Collection Patrick Higson.*
Photograph   Victor Albrow)

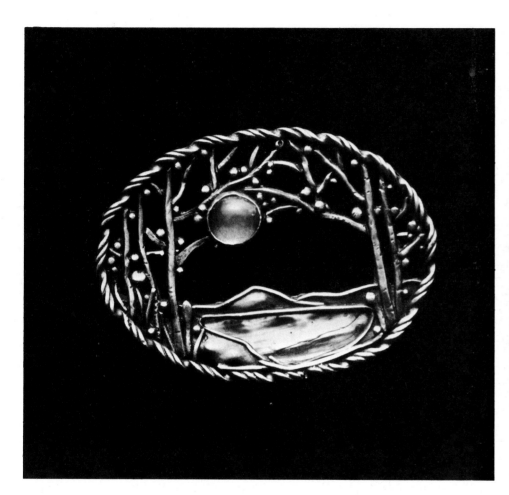

195. Another piece of jewellery by Mary Thew.

196. An exquisitely enamelled, very tiny, brooch attributed by the present owner to Jessie King, who rarely achieved such an affinity with the early work of the Four.
(*Collection Mrs Sturrock.*
Photograph   Victor Albrow)

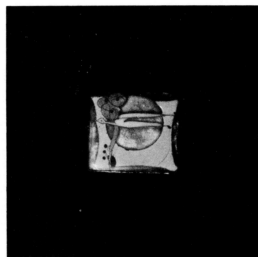

197, 198. Two silver and enamel buckles made by Liberty and Co., one hallmarked 1908, the other 1906, designed by Jessie King, with her birds, her flowers, and her characteristic use of the tiny square motif.
(*Collection Irina Laski.*
Photograph   Stephen Daniels)

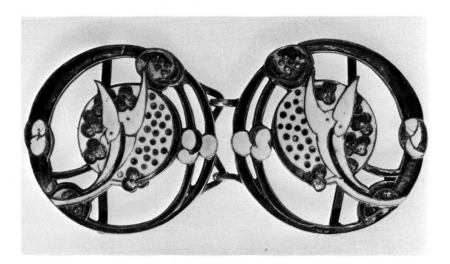

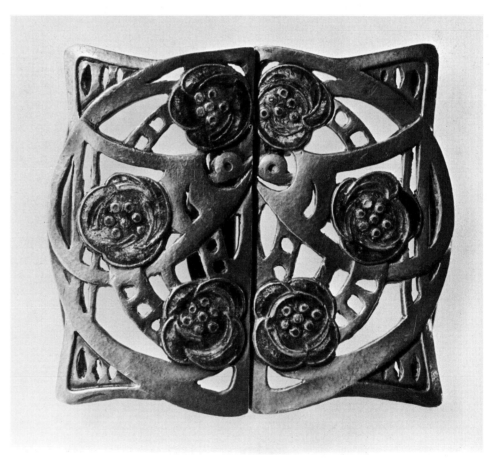

199. This silver and enamel dish, also made by Liberty, is part of a dressing table set, the hairbrush of which is illustrated in *The Studio Yearbook* 1909, where it is attributed to Jessie King.
(*Collection Irina Laski.*
Photograph   Stephen Daniels)

200. There is a certain Glasgow feeling about this silver, enamel and pearl necklace, which appears in the Liberty Sketchbooks in company with the Jessie King jewellery designs, although it could possibly be attributed to Edgar Simpson.
(*Private collection.   Photograph   Victor Albrow*)

201, 202, 203, 204. Four silver and enamel pendants designed by Jessie King for Liberty and Co., all variants of the same theme.
(*Private collection, 201*)
(*Collection Irina Laski, 202, 203*)
(*Collection John Jesse, 204*)
(*Photographs   Stephen Daniels*)

205. Goodbye!
Jessie King in 1939, standing in front of the
green gate that led to her house in Kirkcudbright,
and which was used as a mark on her pottery.